Dancing

Into

Darkness

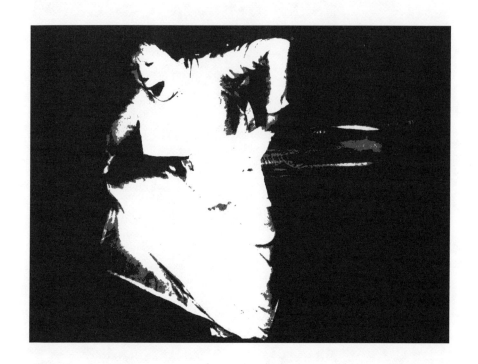

Dancing Into Darkness

Butoh,
Zen,
and
Japan

Sondra
Horton
Fraleigh

University
of
Pittsburgh
Press

Dance
Books

Published by the University of Pittsburgh Press,
Pittsburgh, Pa. 15261,
and Dance Books Ltd.,
15 Cecil Court WC2N 4EZ.

Copyright © 1999, University of Pittsburgh Press

Manufactured in the United States of America
Printed on acid-free paper
10 9 8 7 6 5 4 3 2 1

Frontispiece: Natsu Nakajma in an agonistic passage that precedes the peaceful closure of *Niwa* (*The Garden*). Here the danger transforms into the Goddess Kannon, blending Butoh with Buddhist imagery. *Photograph © Nourit Masson-Sekine.*

Library of Congress Cataloging-in-Publication Data
Fraleigh, Sondra Horton, 1939–
     Dancing into darkness : Butoh, Zen, and Japan / Sondra Horton
Fraleigh
     p. cm.
  Includes bibliographical references and index.
  ISBN 0-8229-4098-1 (cloth : acid-free paper)
  1. Buto. 2. Arts, Zen—Japan. I. Title.
  GV1783.2.B87 F73 1999
  792.8'0952—dc21
                                                    98-58109
                                                    CIP

Dance Books
ISBN 1 85273 068 4

A CIP catalog record for this book is available from the
British Library.

Contents

Acknowledgments xi

Introduction: The Difference the Other Makes 1

Forgotten Garden: Natsu Nakajima's Performance in Montreal 45

The Marble Bath: *Ryokan* in Takayama 55

My Mother: Kazuo Ohno's Class in Yokohama 57

Shibui and the Sublime: Sankai Juku's Performance in Toronto 65

My Mother's Face: Natsu Nakajima's Workshop in Toronto 87

Shards: Saburo Teshigawara's Performance in Toronto 97

Empty Land: Natsu Nakajima's Performance in New York 104

American Mother and Shinto: In Ohno Village 117

Liebe: Susanne Linke and Toru Iwashita 124

Beginner's Body: Yoko Ashikawa's Class in Tokyo 139

Tree: Min Tanaka's Choreography in Tokyo 151

Amazing Grace: Kazuo Ohno's Performance in Yokohama 158

Hot Spring: In Hakone Yumoto 163

The Waters of Life: Kazuo Ohno's Workshop in Yokohama   164

How I Got the Name "Bright Road Friend": With Zen Teacher
    Shodo Akane in Tsuchiura   166

The Existential Answer: Interview with Butoh Critic Nario Goda
    in Tokyo   171

Hokohtai, the Walking Body: Yoko Ashikawa's Performance in
    New York   177

Dance and Zen, *Kyo Ikiru:* With Zen Teacher Shodo Akane in
    Tokyo   180

Prose and Haiku on Japan   186

Post-Butoh Chalk: Annamirl Van der Pluijm's Performance in
    Montreal   195

Dust and Breath: Sankai Juku's Performance in Toronto   199

The Hanging Body: Joan Laage's Performance in Brockport,
    New York   209

Zen and *Wabi-Sabi* Taste: Setsuko Yamada's Performance
    in Toronto   214

The Community Body: Akira Kasai and Yumiko Yoshioka   228

Notes   251

Selected Bibliography   261

Index   265

Illustrations

Tatsumi Hijikata carrying a baby through a field   4

Butoh founder Kazuo Ohno and his son Yoshito   5

Butoh founder Tatsumi Hijikata   7

Playbill for *Kabuki Butoh "Jesus Christ in Aomori"*   16

Sondra Fraleigh and Chiyo Matsumoto-sensei   20

Dairakudakan Butoh company on a playbill for *Tale of the Supernatural Sea Dappled Horse*   27

Kayo Mikami's *Kenka (Consecration of Flowers)*   39

Natsu Nakajima in "The Infant"   49

Natsu Nakajima in "The Ghost"   50

A workshop class at Kazuo Ohno's studio in Yokohama   60

Pina Baush's neo-expressionist *Rites of Spring*   75

Jomon Sho: *Homage to Prehistory*   83

Saburo Teshigawara and Sayoko Yamaguchi in *Ishi-No-Hana (Flower of Stone)*   101

Natsu Nakajima's "Stone Play" from *Empty Land*   109

Natsu Nakajima's "Distant Landscape" from *Empty Land*   113

Natsu Nakajima's "Newspapers" from *Empty Land*   115

Dore Hoyer in "Angst" from *Affectos Humanos*   130

Susanne Linke in *Affecte*   131

Susanne Linke in *Affecte*   133

Toru Iwashita, collaboration with Asuka Kaneko at Ashi Square A
in Tokyo   136

Toru Iwashita, collaboration with Asuka Kaneko at Ashi Square A
in Tokyo   137

Kayo Mikami, Butoh dancer and scholar, in *Kenka*   143

Min Tanaka in *I Sit*   153

Kazuo Ohno in *Suiren* (*Waterlily*)   160

Ryokan fish pond with reflections of the mountains in Hakone   163

Kazuo Ohno and his son Yoshito Ohno   165

Sondra Fraleigh serving tea   167

Tatsumi Hijikata sitting on a fence   172

Akeno Ashikawa and Hakutobo, the Butoh company founded by
Yoko Ashikawa   179

Flower arrangement at Zen temple Zensho-An in Tokyo   183

Self-portrait of Sondra Fraleigh in a traditional Japanese *yukatta*   193

Annamirl Van der Pluijm in *Solo 1*   197

Sankai Juku in *Shijima*   205

Joan Laage in *Nothing Lasts but Memory*   210

Joan Laage in a posture typical of Butoh forms   213

Hanging and Receiving: Setsudo Yamada   221

Portrait of Akira Kasai   229

Akira Kasai improvising   234

Yumiko Yoshioka in *It's All Moonshine*   242

Yumiko Yoshioka demonstrates the disposition of Butoh toward
  visual art and meditative architectures   244

Calligraphy by Zen Teacher and Calligrapher Shodo Akane

The Garden of Life (Willows are green and flowers red)   45

Light of a Stone Lantern (A lantern lights the corner)   55

Mother Goddess (Kind-Mother Kwan-Yin, the female Buddha)   57

Meeting of Birth and Death (Life and death are the same)   65

Original Face (Be a master wherever you are)   87

Flower of Stone (Thousands of flowers carved in rock)   97

Empty Land (All is nothing)   104

Dragon (Dragon)   117

Love (Love)   124

Beginner's Body (Born kindness is everlasting)   139

Tree (Rite of wood)   151

Grace (Kindness of grass)   158

Onsen, Hot Spring (Bathing your body and heart)   163

Waters of Life (Morning clouds and flowing water)   164

Bright, oh Bright, oh Bright (Bright, *bright,* **bright**)   166

Darkness (Ink-bars contain thousands of colors)   171

Hokohtai, the Walking Body (Feeling free in movement)   177

Kyo Ikiru, Live Today (One day reflects one life)   180

Green Land (Green land and yellow gold)   186

Footprints (Buddha's foot-stone)   195

Dust and Breath (Not a single thing)   199

Unconscious Mind (With no mind)   209

Wabi-Sabi, Plain and Austere Beauty (Slow breeze and bright moon)   214

Unidentified (Left open to the imagination)   228

The calligraphy titles listed above are the author's requests to Shodo Akane-sensei for his calligraphy to represent the chapters of the book. The phrases that follow in parentheses are translations of Akane-sensei's calligraphy as read by Chinese calligrapher Yong Shi.

Acknowledgments

I want to thank my Zen teacher Shodo Akane-sensei for the calligraphy that introduces each section of this book. *Sensei*, as many Westerners know, is an honorific and respectful term for teacher. Akane-sensei is a master teacher of Zen, although not a monk. His Zen mastery is calligraphy, considered the most difficult and highest art in Japan and China. He has also written more than two hundred books on Zen, illustrated with his calligraphy.

I met him through Akiko Akane, a friend I made in Japan who just happened (lucky for me) to be his daughter. I am grateful to both of them for their friendship and support. I tell the story of my meeting with Akane-sensei in the chapter, "How I Got the Name 'Bright Road Friend.'" During a later visit with Akane-sensei, I became interested in what his other students were like, so I asked him. He said that most of his students were business groups who want to integrate Zen principles and spirituality into their work. He finally laughed, and said: "My students are Japanese businessmen, and one American dancer."

When I asked more recently if he would make calligraphy for my book on *Butoh, Zen, and Japan,* he answered: "Yes, with joy!" The calligraphy is intended to be a statement of its own in relation to the poetic/imagistic essence of the text. It bears no direct relationship to Butoh, since Akane-sensei has never seen this particular form of dance arising from the unique issues of postwar Japan. He has placed great trust in me as I proceed in this project. When I fear I don't deserve this and begin to apologize in his presence, he gets bored. As I recount my faults, he repeats: "It is human," over and over, until we both get bored and move to more interesting topics. He is definitely not interested in confessions. He always wants to know what I am thinking and dancing about.

He learned that I carried a stone for twenty minutes in my dance *Meditations* that was performed in Japan in 1992. He could not come to see the dance but asked me about it. I told him I carried a heavy stone and walked so slowly and smoothly as to barely be moving while others were dancing with rhythmic punctuations and thematic variations in space. I created a still point for their dance (that I hoped would disappear in slow time). He stood up suddenly when I told him about the stone and told me I should write about dance and Zen. I told him that the idea for the stone had come from my acquaintance with *Noh* dance (a Zen form) and the influence of Butoh, and that I didn't feel qualified to write about Zen. He ordered me to.

"First write ten pages and send it to me," sensei said. "Write ten, and then you'll write a hundred." I wrote ten and sent them.

Now his calligraphy graces my writing in this text. I haven't counted the pages that relate to Zen. This would be difficult; it is woven in where it seems to apply. It is entirely sensible to include calligraphy in a book about Dance, Zen, and Japan—for it speaks to all three. Calligraphy is like dance; it communicates in images, and its messages are not mediated in words. It can cross language barriers, even as it has some basis in language making. Ultimately it is a free form of expression, just as dance is. Calligraphy is the dance of the hand of the master. His character and innocence in the moment, his beginner's mind, is communicated. It is in this spirit that I joyfully include Akane-sensei's Zen calligraphy and gratefully acknowledge the one piece of advice he ever gave me: "Every day be beautiful."

(I have come to understand this in two ways. I can call my days to me and make them beautiful, or find the beauty in myself. Finally, there is no way to separate the two ideas. They both ensue from consciousness. Akiko, his daughter, told me that his statement also means, "Every day find peace.")

I would also like to thank Janice La Pointe-Crump for her commentary on an early version of the text, and Sarah Watts and Judith Kitchen for editorial elucidation. My travels in Japan have been greatly facilitated by Chiyoe Matsumoto-sensei, Chio Kawaguchi, Fumie Kanai, and Harumi Morishita. I can never thank them enough. As always, I am grateful for the support of my family and the dance community in upstate New York—my colleagues of twenty-six years in the SUNY Brockport Department of Dance, and just as many years of inspiring students.

Dancing

Into

Darkness

Introduction

June 17, 1997

This metaphysical diary on *Butoh, Zen, and Japan* is undertaken in the spirit of the difference the other can make. As a student of Zen and Butoh, I have set forth a diary of essays and poetry that explores and savors my changes in apprehension—metaphysical and aesthetic. Inhaling my otherness, I witnessed my own unfolding and transformation in Japan. In setting down my thoughts, I found I had collected experiences, not the objects of art themselves. They marked my path on a larger journey, the dance of which we are all a part. When I left America, I remember a friend saying to me: "Japan will change your life." She knew I was in for more than theatrical and cultural sightseeing.

The essays in this volume begin a chronology that led me to

this journey. They carry through it and continue with reflections back, reworking and integrating aesthetic points of view and new understandings through ongoing study. My metaphysical journeying in Japan through Zen and Butoh is still unwinding. Meanwhile Butoh has moved from marginal theater to center stage in recent performances at major and regional theaters in Japan and around the world. Artists like Yoko Ashikawa who once performed for Butoh-identified audiences finally achieved wider recognition in Japan and abroad, also performing at the Joyce Theater in New York City. Kazuo Ohno, who turned ninety years old in 1996, is still performing internationally. In America, he performed the entire cycle, *My Mother*, at the Japan Society in New York in February 1996, prancing to an Elvis Presley recording of a Baptist hymn for his encore. Critic Camille Hardy called the encore "an obscene afterthought" to the dance, but she also detailed Ohno's "unusual physical beauty and visual mysticism, now only fleetingly seen in live performance."[1]

Does all this mean that Butoh has become mainstream? No, I don't think so. For many, its novel mixtures of aesthetic means will continue to seem "obscene." Existing in the cultural cracks, Butoh intends to be jarring and (like the sound of one hand clapping) provocative.

If not mainstream, it has become a very large stream indeed, and it has had the powerful aesthetic result of erasing cultural differences between "us" and "them." While politicians continue to fight for territorial turf internationally, Butoh dancers are bridging cultures. Natsu Nakajima has created works for American,

Canadian, and French dancers. (I describe one of these in "Empty Land.") Min Tanaka has recently undertaken *The Poe Project*, based on stories by Edgar Allen Poe with a libretto by Susan Sontag. This project will include U.S.-based dancers who will live on Tanaka's farm in Japan while the dance work is being completed. More intrinsically, Butoh itself crosses cultural boundaries, as we shall take up in various contexts.

Butoh anticipates a growing global amalgamation of previous distinctions: racial, cultural, and aesthetic.[2] It shows Japan's historical/spiritual ties with other Asian countries in its contemplative movement modes. Butoh also unsettles traditional gender distinctions and East/West differences in its eclectic use of music and costumes. As the twenty-first century dawns, it is becoming more difficult to trace pure identities, and Butoh celebrates this fact even as it asserts a Japanese essence. Its beauty stems from its search for corporeal universals amid folk roots.

Dancing into darkness: the stories, essays, and poetry of this text also cross boundaries, but they all derive either directly or implicitly from the mythical feminine (*yin*), the dark earth principle at work in the Butoh aesthetic. My explorations of Butoh, also called "the dance of darkness," have led me to a deeper appreciation of Zen and Japan, which I have woven into these essays. The aesthetics of Butoh reflect the older values of pre-modern Japan. They evoke the original face of Japan beneath the fast-paced surface, and the timeless austerity of Zen, awash with mystical emptiness and nature's evanescence.

If Butoh contains a Zenlike spirit, it is also unmistakably post-

Tatsumi Hijikata, carrying a baby through a field. From Eikoh Hosoe's photography book on Hijikata and his performance of *Kamaitachi* (1969). *Photo © Eikoh Hosoe.*

modern, an arresting aesthetic jumble of historical periods and cross-cultural bodies. But Butoh is more than collage. Its collisions explore a Japanese identity in folk and spiritual traditions (Shinto and Zen) and subvert the West's commercial influence.

Butoh has been growing and diversifying in styles since its inception in 1959 with Tatsumi Hijikata's homoerotic performance of *Kinjiki* (Forbidden Colors). Without music or conventional dance movement, he danced this on a darkened stage as a duet with Yoshito Ohno, Kazuo Ohno's son. Hijikata's deviation from

Butoh founder Kazuo Ohno and his son Yoshito improvise for a photograph by Kevin Bubriski. Ohno's upward gaze focuses our attention on
his eyes while Yoshito's eyes are hidden. Ohno's fingers articulate an intimate inner space while Yoshito's fingers tense into claws.

established aesthetics shocked a Japanese dance community that had been for many years cultivating Western modern dance forms. Butoh, through Hijikata (1928–1986) and its other founder, Kazuo Ohno (b. 1906), developed a primal form of dance theater that continues to evolve. It has also inspired corporeal environmental art through performers like Min Tanaka, whose clothed and nude body has been photographed extensively as he moves trancelike in juxtaposition with a wide variety of natural and manmade environments, including the extremes of Iceland, where he painted his body black, and construction sites with steel girders as background for dramatic costumes. Butoh takes a distinctly different turn from the matter-of-fact minimalism and mundane playfulness of American postmodern dance that also began in the 1960s. Butoh taps the subconscious body by stripping the social body, and its aesthetic dramatizes the beauty of emergent form through natural processes of birth and decay.

Butoh is at once natural and theatrical. It is now more an aesthetic movement than a specific dance or theater form, also inspiring a great deal of photography and visual art. Pittsburgh artist Robert La Bobgah has designed a large *Hijikata Triptych* with shadowy painting and poetry that captures Butoh's concern with death and the void. Recent choreography influenced by Butoh such as that of Setsuko Yamada downscales the shock of the original Butoh daring. In her contemporary work and others, there is a postButoh break with Butoh origins that nevertheless builds upon its movement techniques and descendant values of darkness. There are also artists who continue to expand upon Hijikata's original

Butoh founder Tatsumi Hijikata on the right panel of the *Hijikata Triptych* by Pittsburgh artist Robert La Bobgah, also photographed by La Bobgah. He states his interest in "the darkness that our modern eye has lost, where the gap between words and things disappear." "I shake hands with the dead," is how Hijikata expresses his central thematic.

style—such as American Joan Laage and Japanese Kayo Mikami. Butoh has branched out from its beginnings to become international in its productions and its appeal as well as its choreographers and dancers. In producing a novel fusion of worldcut fragments, Butoh may be the most intercultural postmodern art we have (if the labels *postmodern* and *Butoh* have not become too limiting).

Butoh might also be viewed as part of the restoration of the expressionist origins of modern dance in the postmodern period, paralleling but diverging significantly from the developments of contemporary Tanztheater in Germany arising through Pina Bausch, Susanne Linke, and others. Butoh and Tanztheater both have sources in the original expressionist movement in Germany, as we shall take up. In any case, it is not possible to entirely separate Butoh from any of these movements. It represents an important development in the growth of modern/postmodern dance (even if it rejects extant styles), just as "modern" and "postmodern" are also inextricably linked, yet distinct. Butoh is not an aesthetic movement grafted onto Western dance, and Western dance may be more Eastern than we have been able to see. Butoh helps us to understand the global development and borrowings of modern/postmodern dance.

We should especially note that the original modern dance through Ruth St. Denis, Mary Wigman, and Martha Graham often turned to Eastern cultures for its inspiration and stylizations, and the passionately lean Ukiyo-e Japanese prints were much admired by the expressionists. If Butoh took part of its impetus from the experimental nature of modern dance, modern dance including its early expressionist school borrowed liberally from the aesthetic styles of the East. Which came first, East or West? Even the terms are too general for an adequate answer. Japan, China, France, Nigeria, Korea, Canada, the United States, Brazil, and more all have distinct (if sometimes overlapping) histories and cultures. At the same time, all are part of one modern cultural and intellectual world.

April 23, 1996

Zen and Japan are folded into my major subject of Butoh—"the dance of utter darkness." As I write, it is now 1996, eleven years since I first saw this unique and astounding dance expression that emerged from postwar Japan. Butoh has now become post-Butoh and beyond, but it has retained an essential expressionist thread akin to the unparalleled Ukiyo-e woodcut color prints, originating in the second half of seventeenth-century Japan. This art, also called "Pictures of the Floating World School," died out with the influence of the West when Japan opened its doors to foreigners in 1868.

Curiously enough the postmodern/neo-expressionist Butoh moved back in time to recover Japan's folk identity in the midst of its rapid westernization after World War II. The master stylists of Butoh have much in common with Ukiyo-e's abstract stylizations of the human figure in motion that are still vital today. Woodcuts illustrated popular life and the original Kabuki theater—its actors and patrons, passions and intrigues. The print colors, now dimmed through age, were once very bright. This art captured the life in Edo (the original name for Tokyo) after the Tokugawa shogunate brought stability and prosperity to a troubled country in the seventeenth century.

Ukiyo-e documents common life as well as the sophistications and vices of the times. Many prints concern the world-within-a-world of the queenly courtesans of the Green Houses. Heroic legends and historical romances dealing with the civil wars of the middle ages abound. Depictions often employ a traditional Japanese feminine grace. Suzuki Harunobu, who died in 1770, painted "Eight Parlour Scenes" (1766) and "Girl Performing the 'Lion Dance'" (1769–70). His pupil Harushige painted "Courtesan Leading a Youth to her Bed with a Lighted Taper whilst her Young Attendant Sleeps" (1772). Torii Kiyomine (1787–1869), a master of the Torii school, was one of the last of this great line of Japanese artists. His subject, "Geisha Restringing her Samisen" (1807), would be typical. There are also rural scenes of travelers on the road, families and lovers, and daily activities like washing clothes. Its subjects are wide-ranging, but play, sex, and theater—not work—are the serious occupations of Ukiyo-e.

Katsukawa Shunko was one of the earliest Ukiyo-e artists to design O-kub-e, or large heads, as in his "Head of an *Onnagata*" (1787). An *onnagata* is a male actor taking female parts in the Kabuki. Butoh scholar Susan Blakeley Klein notes that in its beginnings, Butoh sought to bring its expression within the original popular mass appeal of Kabuki before it became refined for

Western taste. Butoh also appropriated early Kabuki exploration of the dark and repressed sides of social life and its ability to turn this into an aesthetic positive.[3]

Nature was another thematic in the development of wood-block color prints, as it later would be in Butoh. In Ukiyo-e as in Butoh, worldliness and high theatricality exist alongside nature and the bucolic. Costumes are a preoccupation in both arts. The body is elaborately adorned in both Ukiyo-e and Butoh, or exposed and boldly colored with paint and white powder. Ukiyo-e, like Butoh, is not remote from Western sensibilities. The aesthetic climate of the expressive Ukiyo-e style is more accessible to us than earlier, more formal and distanced Japanese art.[4] Ukiyo-e's stylized emotions can be recognized in consummate Butoh faces, in love, hopelessness, terror, even ferocity—then in stillness—so beautiful that one holds one's breath.

Affectivity in Butoh (as in Ukiyo-e) is concentrated and exaggerated, an important element of its communicative power. Indeed, the emotional intensity of Butoh proves an example of aesthetic and social rebellion, drawing up a dualistic Japanese history, anything but puritanical, of behavioral tolerances and violations juxtaposed with a gentle fastidiousness and quiet grace. There is great ambiguity in both Ukiyo-e and Butoh. Significantly, Butoh holds parody, travesty, cross-dressing, and burlesque in common with Ukiyo-e.[5] These can be seen in Hijikata's outrageous dance, *Revolt of the Flesh* (1968).

A more recent inspiration for Japan's avant garde theater, whose first major figure was Hijikata, comes from the late Meiji, Taisho, and early Showa period popular art, the mass art of roughly 1910–1930. Japanese film critic Donald Richie describes this movement as developing a novel vocabulary that pictured better "or at least more innocent" days through bright colors, cartoon hard-edge drawings, menus, newspapers, old photographs, and abundant depictions of extreme emotions that turned on a purposeful naivete.[6] This time period corresponds with the root development of expressionist modern art (and dance) in Europe and America, but was more a pop-art movement in Japan.

During the fifties and into the sixties, Hijikata presented theatrical performances unlike any seen in postwar Japan or anywhere else. In startling bad taste, he brandished an oversized strapped-on penis, then danced in a pink dress with knee socks —his wild lion hair, beard, and mustache adding an absurdly dadaist touch or *Taisho-look*. I saw this dance on film at the Museum of Modern Art in San Francisco at an installation on Hijikata's work in the summer of 1996. There were no chairs, so I assumed a typical Asian sitting posture on the floor, and my husband Warren leaned against the wall. (Like many American men, his legs won't fold into the sitting posture.) I watched people come and go throughout, staying for no more than minutes at a time, then leaving in embarrassed silence. Many covered their mouths or eyes, or looked at the floor. Warren and I were the only ones to see the whole performance. Hijikata, part shaman, part deconstructor, groped toward a new dance form that would bridge popular and esoteric art worlds as he lamented the death of Japan.

Hijikata's clashing *Taisho-look* seen in early Butoh experiments is now transforming or disappearing, having served as a shock awakening, but the love of design and distillation of emotion demonstrated in Ukiyo-e continues to pour through the opening that the original Butoh created. In Butoh and Ukiyo-e, emotion is unforgettably etched in face and figure. We can also find convincing etching (or stylization) of emotion in German expressionism (Mary Wigman, Kurt Jooss, and Harald Kreutzberg) and early modern dance in America (especially Martha Graham). The Butoh face, however, is magnified; it dances in minute detail as in Ukiyo-e. In Ukiyo-e's stylizations, everything dances, even the kimonos and butterflies dance, and moths have been etched in flight. Neither Ukiyo-e nor Butoh is limited in aesthetic range or detail. Kobu Shunman, 1757–1820, uses silvery grays and light touches of soft colors to paint miniature creatures and state their significance in *Hawk-Moth and Butterflies*, just as founding Butoh artist and teacher Kazuo Ohno considers the universe in moth wings and explores embryonic dance, *A Dream of the Fetus*, in a softly detailed and inner-directed style that is the reverse side of Hijikata's wildness.

Ohno traces his relationship with his feminine side in *My Mother*. Remembering the womb, he explores control, desire, and exertion in a section called "The Will." He feels his mother's presence with him after death in "I Shall Not Correct It." I was lucky to see Ohno's impromptu performance of this dance in his studio, and to experience the movement he inspires in students from this source, as I describe in the chapter, "My Mother." Ohno was to provide Hijikata's raw confrontational style a gentle complement. Even so, Ohno teaches that to know the universe, we cannot turn away from ugliness and the messy refuse of life.

Ohno and Hijikata both grew up poor, as the conscience and dark poiesis of their dancing reflects. They say they dance with death and the ancestors invoking the spirits of their mothers and sisters, or as Hijikata states it: "When I am immersed in creating a dance my sister scratches away the darkness inside me / finally devouring it all." Hijikata died at midlife, while Ohno, in his nineties, is the oldest living Butoh soloist and still performs his poetic choreography internationally.

Butoh has sought (and is still unraveling) what is most essentially Japanese. I hope to show, however, that the deeper search of Butoh is for what it means to be human. As I documented my experiences in Butoh workshops and performances, my appreciation of Zen meditation and Butoh aesthetics grew. I began to see a Zen emptiness and cathartic aesthetic at work in the development of Butoh, one not culturally or historically circumscribed. Through the 1980s and nineties, I began to notice that Butoh was also becoming an international movement, that it held a universal touchstone for many. Now, wherever I go, I am learning about Butoh-influenced dance and theater; in Canada, the United States, Britain, France, Germany, Brazil, and most recently in Norway with the Butohbasert group of Monica Emilie Herstad. Susannah Akerlund carries on the tradition of Yoko Ashikawa in Sweden, and San Francisco hosts an annual international Butoh festival through d-net (dance-network) and Dancers' Group. When we in the Congress on Research in Dance overlapped our 1993 conference with the Association of American Theater in Higher Education in Atlanta, they had more sessions on Butoh than we did.

As I traveled the Japanese character through Butoh in Japan, I realized that some of the postmodern dance that had caught my attention earlier in America in the 1970s had a Butoh basis unknown to me at the time. These flashed back in sudden recognition: Kei Takei with her explorations of a collective unconscious (why did she tap and slam rocks together, and pile them in circles?), and the hypnotic Eiko and Koma (why did their slow and minimal erotic duets feature potatoes?). In Japan, where Butoh has had a most difficult struggle for acceptance, this year saw an unprecedented collaboration between Butoh and Kabuki artists produced by Japan's top Kabuki historian, Masakatsu Gunji: *Kabuki Butoh "Jesus Christ in Aomori."* This work was danced by the famous Kabuki actor/dancer, Kyozo Nakamura, and Butoh performer Yukio Waguri, one of the most technically versatile dancers in Butoh. (Waguri's performance with Natsu Nakajima is detailed in the chapter "Empty Land.") In Gungi's production, Butoh, a radical art in a traditionally conservative country, melded with recent Kabuki, the form it had once rejected (or preserved and transformed in drawing upon its bawdy folk origins). This performance kept alive the spiritual, international, and syncretic flavor of Butoh, taking the crucified Christ as a central figure. If this seems like too much to balance in one theater work, suffice it to say that balance has not been the mainstay of Butoh's multicultural expressionism.

Playbill advertisement for *Kabuki Butoh "Jesus Christ in Aomori,"*
produced by Masakatsu Gunji, one of Japan's most respected
critics, and a scholar of both Kabuki and Butoh. Traditional
Kabuki actor/dancer Kyozo Nakamura and Butoh dancer
Yukio Waguri performed. *Photograph by Masakatsu Gunji, used with
permission of Theater X.*

I have not labored to connect these essays, but like a post-modern choreographer or a deconstructive architect, I leave these pathways to the reader's discovery. The essays are based on the experiences of an American in a culture not her own, who has made aesthetic and spiritual ties. When we experience ourselves through another cultural lens, we are enriched. When we interpret another culture through our own lens, we bring the difference the other can bring—sometimes the same things that insiders see, but more often aspects that bridge the known with the strange. And it is the strangeness of the unknown (how it can rearrange our perceptual field) that calls us to travel across the bridge of difference, after all. Then, when familiar territory is given up, the traveler can stand in a new familiar, in the place where worlds (and they are whole worlds) meet.

Late November 1994

My interests often elicit good-natured comments from the Japanese on how it takes a foreigner (who comes to Japan) to "teach the Japanese" about Zen and Butoh. When outsiders take an interest in another culture, especially if they adopt aspects that ring (in some way) true to their own character, natives may see themselves in a new light. Strangeness, the difference the other makes, sharpens the familiar.

I know this happens to me on home ground. When Japanese-born Hidenori Tomozoe, a judo expert, saw an Elizabeth Streb

dance concert with me in America in 1989, he drew an unusual relationship of her work to judo, one I would not have made myself. Streb was once a student of mine, and I had seen her work grow and change over the years, but seeing it through Tomozoe's eyes brought something new to me. Through him, I saw how the split-second single-mindedness of martial arts can appear in dance contexts, generating a gamelike focus (or turn violent as Streb's works later did). I understood the power of full presence—that being fully oriented in present time lends aesthetic power as well as physical strength to dance. In life, as well, keen attention allows one to ride the wave of the present moment. When Chiyoe Matsumoto visited me in upstate New York, my consciousness of my own situation also changed.

Matsumoto-sensei is noted as the founder of dance education in Japanese schools and universities and is a leader in dance research, receiving the Order of the Precious Crown Butterfly from the emperor on November 15, 1993. At seventy-four she is the only woman to receive this highest decoration given to researchers. I became acquainted with her through writing about her life,[7] and she adopted me (in a playful mood) as her American daughter. Many dance educators in Japan were once Matsumoto-sensei's students and call themselves the daughters of Matsumoto, as the arts are often passed along through family tradition in Japan. I was concerned to treat my mother well on her visit. In fact, I had been planning it for a year and a half, as the tea ceremony is planned extensively over time, the host going to great lengths through the ceremony to welcome the guest.

I was very nervous about her visit, knowing full well that I had been treated royally on my visits to Japan. As it turned out, she and three other guests (some of my Japanese sisters) navigated every twist and turn so spontaneously that I actually enjoyed my own party. They sang Japanese songs on our long drive to Niagara Falls—folk songs and children's songs. When I became tired of driving and had to get out of the car, they gave me emergency roadside *shiatzu* massage. (Onlookers must have thought I was being attacked by tourists.)

So much for Japanese reserve. Yes, there was much bowing during their visit, but also much hugging. And they say the Japanese don't hug? Well, maybe not so much in Japan? But new scenery and situations can elicit new responses—fields of ripe pumpkins and the clear fall air of rural New York are anything but Tokyo. I don't know what Matsumoto-sensei's photo record of our trip to Niagara Falls will look like. Our group became concerned with her particular brand of "high risk" photography, "pop-zen" we began calling it. Just stick the camera out the window and shoot; see what you get. This takes faith. That evening I had planned a dinner at home for my Japanese guests. Of course, the customary Japanese presents came out on their arrival. After present opening and champagne toasts, they began singing folk songs again. Once more I felt like the guest being entertained, not the host, and I remembered that in the tea ceremony, as Matsumoto-sensei has explained to me, both the server and the guests are made beautiful by the ritual. A ceremonial party becomes ritual, life becomes theater, theater becomes art.

Chiyo Matsumoto-sensei, a pioneer of dance education in Japan, gives a tea serving lesson to Fraleigh in her somatics studio in Brockport, New York. In the background is Shodo Akane-sensei's Zen calligraphy—*mu* (emptiness). *Photograph by Chiyo Kawaguchi.*

The difference the other makes spreads both ways. When I go to Japan, Japanese who have never meditated will go for the first time to meditate with me in Zen temples, and not just to be good hosts, they have said. Perhaps they are curious concerning a foreigner's interest in Zen; or maybe they take it as an opportunity to explore latent aspects of themselves already present in the profundity of their traditional life, but hidden beneath the hectic Western surface of Japan.

Likewise, Japanese who are devoted to Zen meditation have also experienced it anew when we have meditated together, simply because I represent a difference in their affinity to Zen. I am obviously not an insider. I bring the difference of the other to a long-standing cultural known. This difference can make a difference, as when at a small Zen temple in the mountainous Yumoto Hakone, my friend Akiko Akane and I heard our names chanted together, resounding over the valley.

Akiko, a yoga teacher and Zen meditator, arranged through her father who teaches Zen for our stay in the Maple Leaf Monastery in Hakone, a country town known more for its resorts than temples. It was a crisp chilly morning in early November 1992 when we left the coziness of our *tatami* mat room in the spare *ryokan* (traditional Japanese hotel) on the temple grounds for a morning meditation. The previous night we had soaked in the ryokan's hot mineral baths (white for healing, and red for strength) and enjoyed a simple vegetarian meal served on a polished low table by unspeaking but amiable resident monks in plain dark robes. Before falling asleep on our futons, we watched the valley thicken into blackness, the light of its thousand lanterns and neons spreading out for miles, sloping up to meet the stars on the fading horizon. We were mostly silent, wrapped in our *yukatta* cotton kimonos, the view, and the music of Akiko's friend, Kogo Takashi. He had come with us and brought along a tape of his compositions blending Asian bamboo instruments, computer synthesizer, and sounds from nature.

Before dawn, we walked up the hill for an early morning ceremony and meditation in the small wooden temple at the top of the grounds. It was still dark when we began our sitting, and the temple door was open to the cold morning air. The altar was more ornate than I had been accustomed to, and the ceremony was carried out by a priest richly robed in purple, white, and gold. At the end of the ceremony, light was just dawning in a mist over Hakone, and Akiko and I were the only two meditators remaining in the temple.

Immobile in the cold, we looked at each other in amazement and wonder as our names were added audibly to the chant. What events had brought us from different sides of the world to be sitting there together on this morning, our names forever woven together in a sacred chant? And why had we remained there in the cold for so long after others had gone off to breakfast? Had Akiko stayed behind for me? Was my determination to sit through the cold to the end of the long ceremony spurred by the fact that I might never return to this place? Or had I stayed out of reverence? I remember being transfixed, held there, not wanting to go, not feeling the cold. The memorable collusion was a synthesis of time, place, and persons. To hear our names chanted so unexpectedly out the wide open doors of the temple, the sound floating over the sleeping valley, bound us together in awe. Such experiences of the other, another culture or another person, change us fundamentally. In that moment, I felt my molecules rearranging, and my being formed all over again.

My pursuit of Butoh has also brought "difference" as such into the foreground. But different as Butoh is for me, it is also an art that I recognize as blurring cultural distinctions. As a dance form that grew out of aesthetic upheaval and identity crisis in postwar Japan, Butoh reached a high point of development amid the radical ferment of the sixties. Its times are my times. The globe is getting smaller, and news and aesthetics travel fast. Butoh's costumes are both Eastern and Western, as is its music. Its basic appeal is through the body, the primal body *simpliciter*, reduced to basic concrete gestures and somatically derived techniques.

Butoh has much in common with the devolution of technical polish in American postmodern dance as it arose in the 1960s. But Butoh, unlike the objective pedestrian style of the American postmodern, is expressionist; and it speaks a nature that is Japanese in several ways. Butoh has a flair for the theatrical (the adorned and painted body), and is unashamed of nudity as in premodern (pre-Western) Japan. It consciously tends nature (the nature of the body in this case), subverting the cultural body. Butoh explores awkwardness and organic simplicity, recultivating the body on new and often minimalist terms, as a flower arrangement uses elements from nature and represents them to make the most of the fewest elements (even weeds).

Butoh exists in mythological time. It could be any time, because characterization never solidifies. There is a continual transmogrification of the image. Like meditational time, time in Butoh is always *Now*. It unfolds states of being, eliciting a soul depth that only meditative distillations of slow time can render. In its temporal dimension, Butoh posits these traditional Japanese aesthetic values. Butoh can be elaborate, but it is more often spare, deliberately unhurried, and startling. Like Zen, its slow patience can bring surprise. While Japanese in genesis, Butoh is not culturally bound to Japanese imagery. It crosses over cultural borders, unmasking the culturally mannered body, removing traditional Japanese garments, or weaving them into a modern mosaic, as when Kazuo Ohno's untied yellow kimono trails behind him in *Waterlilies* (1987). He inches forward, using his gnarled walking stick. As his kimono drops and falls away, his aged, almost naked body becomes his costume. In the next moment, his son Yoshito (moving to the music of Pink Floyd) appears, stiff and staccato, in a Western business suit. They are not characters in a play or even an inner drama; they are impressions that pass by and transform in space and time, like Monet's *Waterlilies*, which inspired the dance.

It took time for Butoh to gain recognition in its own country. This is often the fate of new aesthetic movements (Isadora Duncan was first appreciated in Europe, not America). Now Butoh is more generally accepted in Japan as a unique international export. It seems refreshingly other to me, but still close. It speaks directly through the expressive body we all share and is not as removed from contemporary life through centuries of aesthetic overlay as are Kabuki and Noh theater, much as we still enjoy these traditional arts. My association with Butoh has renewed my participation in contemporary dance as a writer and as a teacher/choreographer.

Through Butoh, I have in a curious way revisited aspects of my involvement in German expressionism as a student at the Mary

Wigman School in Berlin (1964–65). It also has recalled my studies in the United States with Martha Graham and Hanya Holm, and dancing with Don Redlich in Holm's works, her extensions of German expressionism in America. Butoh and early expressionism have much in common, however distinct they may be. They both stem from moody dark emotions, and they have dramatic catharsis as their unstated purpose. They are therapeutic, without being explicitly undertaken as such.

Greek tragedy also has catharsis as one of its main elements. Without this transformational element, Greek tragedy would cease to be what it is in essence. Likewise, catharsis is at the aesthetic heart of Butoh, the reason behind its exposure of clumsiness, its distorted faces, and sublime emptying of the self. "Killing the body," they call it. Like Dogen Zen, Butoh "casts off the body and the mind." It plays between emptiness and form, light and dark, beauty and ugliness in its cathartic transformations of the body, tendering the Eastern metaphysical origins of Zen. The Buddhist and Taoist concept of the Way represents such reversible flows: the intermingling of light and dark, of ugliness and beauty. The Way of Tao has a water logic that is not judgmental. "Water goes to places detested by men, its goodness benefits everyone" (Tao Te Ching).

Similarly, the "third eye," a mystical image for seeing beyond opposites, or "beyond good and evil" (as Nietzsche put it in his philosophy),[8] is often developed in Butoh workshops (as I discuss in recounting my experiences with Natsu Nakajima and Yoko Ashikawa). The third eye is most keenly cultivated in the chakra system of Indian yoga. There it is also called "the blue pearl," bliss. Yoga—"the mother of Zen"—as my Zen teacher Shodo Akane-sensei has called it, is a psychophysical discipline sustaining a metaphysics of bodymind unity, the song of the infinite body. Akane-sensei states the oneness principle plainly for Zen: "Body and Mind are One" (Shin Shin Ichijo). In Zen, the body is mindful. In yoga, the body is free from strife and inwardly composed, eye of infinite time and no ambition.

Yoga postures are often depicted erotically, as the life-sustaining sculptures decorating Hindu temples demonstrate. They celebrate the sacred pleasure of unification, eroticism, and spirituality in harmony. The lusty and vibrant Butoh company, Dairakudakan, stirs up a yoga eroticism in its supple and burning *Tale of the Supernatural Sea Dappled Horse*. I saw this in Tokyo in the spring of 1990, in Asakasa, the old section of Tokyo. The theater had been overbooked, so I sat on balcony steps, packed shoulder to shoulder with others, a situation the Japanese are used to—and sometimes expect in the theater. The dance's references to India were unmistakable. They stood out in Dairakudakan's Butoh-jumble of imagery from Japan, India, and the West. Blue/black painted figures with gold crowns, white socks, and ballet slippers danced sinuously, dripping with white painted lines and dappled blotches. The third eye was painted with the symbolic red dot on the forehead.

I saw this as a Shiva/Shakti dance of creation/destruction. Over time, it crystallized yogic poses and lotus hand gestures at odd and surprising moments. The dance unraveled from an ear-

Dairakudakan Butoh company represented in a cross-cultural collage on a playbill advertisement for their work, *Tale of the Supernatural Sea Dappled Horse*, performed in Tokyo in 1990.

splitting opening as dancers are caught in a web of thin rope held fast between their teeth with red rags tied along the expanse. As they are drawn agonistically forward from the background, the rope cuts into the wretched tangle of bodies. Their mouths drop agape, then shake in silent screams as the red cloths, like tongues of fire, are spit out. In the midst of this appears a figure with one giant breast. Here is the messy generative feminine in pastiche. And how is the dancing? Or can you find it underneath the pain and drama? The dancing comes from elastic yogic bodies. It is easy to find, and riveting. Dairakudakan could be criticized for its clashingly overwrought contrasts, but it is impossible to turn away from. It is also a good example of Butoh's cross-cultural fusion-body, and the rebellion of the body in the absurdist *Taisho-look*, not yet dead.

From its surface, it would be hard to get a Zen essence from Dairakudakan. But I am reminded that Zen is tolerant of the irrational and is not interpreted as a religion with dogma. It is essentially a meditative practice. "We're not sure we have religion" they like to say in Zen: "*We Dance.*" Zen acknowledges a dance of stillness where movement and silence meet and the controlling mind is released. Zen and yoga have a bond, but not so much in aesthetic style. Zen is plain, except for its exquisite gardens, and even these are stylized to show simple elements of greenery, water, and rock clearly arranged for the eye and spirit. It is at the bodily level that Zen and yoga meet. Yogic exercises are often used to prepare for the meditational practices and sitting postures of Zen, as I experienced at the Zen Center in Rochester, New York, and in a class on Zen meditation at a temple in Nara, Japan.

Therapeutic reversibility of polarized or tensional elements appearing in Butoh aesthetics is not restricted to an Eastern metaphysics—whether this be the *tan* (tension) of Sanskrit and yoga, the *yin/yang* interplay of Taoism, or the interface of *fullness/emptiness* in Buddhism. A yin/yang reversibility also applies to Western creation myths. Pre-Socratic Greek cosmology posited the generation of life (and all things) as an oscillation between oppositions, night and day, hot and cold, male and female, and so on. From just this perspective, Nietzsche developed "eternal return," at the cosmological core of his philosophical poetry.

There is in the manner of Butoh a more aromatic and tactile cosmology at work. Butoh develops images of smoky incense curling upward around the body, hair floating backward on a river, and Haley's comet tracking across the sky. It mixes these with mundane acts in stages of metamorphosis, such as threading a needle, carrying a cup, or wringing a towel. Transformations from a beautiful woman into a crone are typical in Butoh. These occur as disquieting transmogrifications and might also take place between animal and human bodies, or imagined as thousands of bugs attacking the body: moving through the pores, around the eyes and in the organs, bugs eating bugs, the condition eating itself, eating consciousness, itching into spasms, returning the body to forgetfulness and the flesh, five hundred million bugs eating a tree (consciousness eaten by bugs/sense of material remains).[9] Such images can flow in reversible improvised linkages and are included in Hijikata's descriptive dance notation at the root of Butoh. Since Hijikata's death, the images continue to be explored in the classes of Yoko Ashikawa, Natsu Nakajima, and Kayo

Mikami who all worked with Hijikata and were led by his enor-
mously varied and colorful verbal expressions. Hijikata choreographed through a poiesis that was so complex it prompted a
professor of Japanese literature to say "please translate Hijikata
into Japanese."

Kazuo Ohno's imagery, also foundational in Butoh, plays upon
cathartic transformation. His images might come from anywhere,
internally derived or globally: the growth of the fetus, the Dead
Sea, the famous dancer La Argentina, Monet's *Waterlilies* juxtaposed with the music of Pink Floyd and the *Ave Maria*. Ohno is
faithful to a larger scheme always—the world and the body as
cosmos. As he puts it in dance classes: "If you want to understand
your body, walk on the ocean floor. . . . Become moth dust. . . .
The entire universe imprints on the moth's wing."

After its Japanese incubation in the 1960s and 1970s, Butoh
grew internationally, inspiring dance and drama that cultivated
its tragic expressionism and metaphysical transformations on
new grounds, just as American and German modern dance initiated international growth of new dance that would challenge the
traditions of ballet around the world. At first, my interests in seeing Butoh and studying it in Japan often met with polite in-
credulity. How could this American woman, a professor with a
background in modern dance and philosophy, be interested in
Butoh? Butoh seemed a little strange to many of the people I spoke
to. They wondered if I might not like to see Kabuki or Noh, or
even Japanese modern dance, instead. Of course I wanted to see
them all, and also Bunraku (puppet theater) for good measure.

Subsequently, I saw a great deal of Japanese modern dance. I came to understand it as a form developed in Japan from European and American influences, a prime example of the difference the other makes. It grew both in education and professional dance roughly over the same period as contemporary dance in the United States, as Japan opened itself to outside influences in the Meiji era (beginning in 1868). Influenced by the proliferation of ballet and contemporary dance in the twentieth century, modern dance in Japan began to reflect the expressionist beginnings of new dance in the United States and Germany (in the twenties and thirties). Japanese dancers excelled in the subsequent development of more technical, formal, and musically lyrical dance that grew in creative ferment around the globe.

The many performances of modern dance I have seen in Japan since 1990 recall Doris Humphrey's formal, democratic group dynamics, Martha Graham's sculpted motion, and Mary Wigman's appreciation for the poetically symbolic (but with less grip and lighter flow). They are not copies, however, and their choreographic means vary widely. The early growth of modern dance in Japan was strongly influenced by Takaya Eguchi who studied with Mary Wigman in Germany and by Baku Ishii who called his dances poetry or haiku. Ishii studied ballet with the Imperial Theater Company in Tokyo. He also pursued the Dalcroze Technique and German Neue Tanz with his friend Kosaku Yamada upon Yamada's return from Germany.[10]

Eguchi's work with Wigman and Ishii's "haiku" spread two ways in Japan. Through their study and teaching of expressionist modern dance, Eguchi and Ishii lent direction to the development of Japanese concert dance and also provided the link between German expressionism and Butoh.[11] Ohno studied with Ishii in 1933 and Eguchi in 1936, and Hijikata studied German-style modern dance under Katsuko Masumura, a student of Eguchi, and with Mitsuko Ando, a disciple of Eguchi. Ohno and Hijikata met through Ando sometime between 1952 and 1954.[12]

The influence of Japanese choreographer/dancer Michio Ito is also evident in the development of Japanese modern dance. He gained wide recognition early in the twentieth century with much of his work being performed in Europe and the United States, including Hollywood. Ito's melding of the emerging modern dance with Japanese sensibility was greatly admired by Debussy, Rodin, Yeats, and Shaw, and by thousands in the United States, where he danced from 1916 to 1941. He contributed to the emerging dance theater in the United States and its appetite for the exotic in Orientalist stereotypes. In those times, the Oriental was imagined as a "spiritual being" of profound "artistic refinement" coexisting with "the devious, lazy and sensual stereotype."[13]

Ito's dream of melding East and West, spirit and material, employed a unique blend of his Japanese background with his Dalcroze training. The Dalcroze school exalted bodily, psychic, and cosmological integration, as the Asian yin/yang interlocking teardrop symbol over its door shows. Because Ito was "the other," his contributions as an artist influencing and being influenced by developments in early American modern dance were never fully appreciated. His work in Japan after World War II did not focus on his Oriental works, but on clearly defined form and human (universal) themes and emotions. These would closely relate his work to Doris Humphrey's formal dance designs.[14] We also know that Ito experienced music visualization, as a choreographic strategy where he taught at the Denishawn school in the 1920s.

Today, mainstream Japanese modern dance (I also call this concert dance) balances formal structure with lyricism. It abounds with expressive melodic line—unbroken, sustained, and flowing —like the lyricism that came to characterize so much early music visualization and also the later technical phase of modernism in the United States. One of the more balletic renditions of Paul Taylor, *Roses* (composed in 1985 to Richard Wagner's romantic *Siegfried Idyll* and Heinrich Baermann's *Adagio for Clarinet and Strings*) is a good example. Lyric dance (as I see it) is phrased like harmonious music with swells and ebbs, and it moves within graceful parameters of control, whether the movement is fast and strong or gentle. It strives for a natural balance between conscious control and instinct.

Certainly, there are examples that would contradict my attribution of lyricism to Japanese modern dance, especially now that postmodern fragmentation is apparent in many works. Perhaps we should consider postmodern deconstructive developments entering into Japanese concert dance and the rebellion of Butoh as entirely new developments akin to the postmodern in America. The majority of Japanese concert dance (seen in college concerts and professional companies) is still conscious of harmonic flow, clean expressiveness, and ingenious group orchestration. Fumie

Kanai's contemporary company is a good example. It is technically sharp with a grace that cuts through time, exact in each moment. Her dance, *Wind and Wood* (1990), flies, poised in readiness to the end. Phrases finish without finishing; they remain alert. There is sweep and thrill in her dances, lithe beauty slicing the air, and a clear weave of the group over time. It is great dancing, but the opposite of Butoh's gestural, nitty-gritty expressionism. Like Kazuo Ohno, Fumie Kanai was a student of Eguchi, and she was also his assistant for many years; yet Ohno and Kanai are at opposite ends of an aesthetic spectrum.

Through Ohno and Hijikata, and those who followed after them, Butoh challenged extant definitions of concert and theater dance in Japan, whether it be Western-influenced ballet and modern dance like that of Kanai or the homegrown popular Kabuki and classical Noh drama. (In searching out a Japanese essence, the creativity of Butoh would eventually run the gamut from Kabuki's turbulence[15] to Noh's stillness.) Butoh bursts controlled lyricism, expressing the uncontrolled body and pathetic conditions. The collective unconscious is the arena of Butoh's aesthetic. It is extreme in its probings of hidden or dark dimensions of consciousness and the evolutionary human body as emergent animate form. Butoh shows form coming into being. This is especially apparent in Ushio Amagatsu's company, Sankai Juku. Butoh is most of all a process of finding expression, a primal body utterance. Its cathartic field is composed of gestural images rising to form out of the subconscious in whatever sublime or awkward manner they take.

This field is poetized; it is danced, but not in the wake of character development, like early modern dance dramas. These include Graham's queenly Jocasta in *Night Journey* (1947), and the summation of Graham's artistry in *Clytemnestra* (1958), where she explores passion, violence, and redemption through Greek mythology. Some of the earliest dark utterances in dance expressionism come through Germany with Mary Wigman in her *Witch Dance* (the first in 1914 and the second in 1926). Unlike American characterization of mythology and literature, Wigman's images are impressions, not characters. She uses masks to derealize (and universalize) character.

When I studied with Wigman in 1964–65, we were structuring compositions that explored a collective unconscious, although I don't remember her putting it in these terms, since they were often poured through literary classics (but in a less narrative manner than Graham). We choreographed and danced solos based on such characters as Electra and Ophelia, but we didn't dance the characters; we danced the characteristics. I remember that Wigman gave me the problem of composing a dance on Penthesilea, her Amazon powers and contradictions, as described by Henrich von Kleist. (I especially recall the pleasurable strength of a rhythmic stamping section, and smearing my face with gold and red paint.) Our works dwelt not on plot, but on psyche, on archetypes as exemplified in characters: Electra's complex attachment to the father (described by Freud as a reverse Oedipal complex), Ophelia's death wish, and Penthesilea's conflict between her overdetermined and sexually impressible selves.[16] These were not just convenient models; they were fatally female, and Wigman pointed this out.

That one would dance into the soul of a character to expose the raw substance of human psyche was explored in Wigman's school. Dance therapy, while far from Freudian persuasions, developed out of such psychotherapeutic explorations. Improvisation classes at the Wigman school were more directly evocative of inner life than the more lyrically structured, musically guided improvisational problems in my dance studies in the United States. In the German school, one tapped into the psyche, but it was aesthetically represented. Even the children's classes developed "Witch Dances" after drawing the awful creatures. The children's witches were both aesthetically improvised child's play and innocent demonic exorcism. Their therapeutic play allowed the monstrous to cavort.

It is becoming increasingly apparent that German expressionism is a major root of Butoh.[17] I was reminded of this when I took Ohno's workshops in Yokohama. His classes resembled my studies at the Wigman Studio in Berlin. The settings for Wigman and Ohno's classes were both casual and homey, far from institutionalized dance schools in universities and professional studios where students come and go and may even remain anonymous. The Wigman Studio was in an old mansion converted into the Wigman School in Berlin after World War II. The main studio used to be the dining room, and it was small. Ohno's studio was next to his home, a one-room studio with costumes, posters, memorabilia here and there, and tea and fruit.

Ohno developed a pedagogical style that I had also experienced with Wigman. I noted this at the time, even though it was much later that I learned from Ohno's biography of his connections to German expressionism.[18] In Ohno's studio, we students sat at his feet for about a half an hour at the beginning of class while he talked poetically and passionately about the dance theme we would explore. He put us "in the mood," so to speak, for the improvisation to follow. Wigman was also particularly good at stirring the imagination and prompting whole movement studies with her words, as we sat at her feet at the beginning of class. In her classes, as in Ohno's, the students came from various parts of the world.

The resemblance between Ohno and Wigman breaks down in the movement. The movement Ohno elicits is floating and finely detailed with interspersed sudden motivations or awakenings from within. Sometimes the movement is so subtle that it is almost invisible. There is much stillness. His workshops follow a stream of consciousness sparked by his poetic imagery and philosophy. "Butoh is life," Ohno says simply. Life and death are his subjects. He talks of war in its dubious function, how death is intended to contribute to life. And he speaks of reproduction, how many sperm die in the race to fertilize an egg that will become a living being.

Wigman structured improvisations for us to perform, describing strength, weakness, deviousness, and other human attributes. Sometimes she gave short instructions to be fulfilled on the spot, like "surprise me," or "contrast up and down." The contrast was not simply directional, however, as I remember her imperative for our improvisation: "Consider everything in the heavens when you look up and everything that the underworld represents in going down."

"Move very quickly and in a complicated manner," was one of her more abstract instructions. At the Wigman School, we worked on instructions spontaneously, then showed them to the class in various states on their way from improvisation to chore-ography. They were expressively directed, more outwardly dem-onstrated or extroverted than in Ohno's classes. With Ohno one tuned an inner eye to the movement and oneself, aided by the soft music of Japanese harp or flute in the background. (Students would sometimes blur or close their eyes in the process.) The effect could be hypnotic, relaxing, disturbing, and restorative. Ohno's teaching was provocative and nonjudgmental. In his studio one could revisit what psychology now calls "the inner child."

This delicate attunement to the remembered and subtle body is a major difference between Butoh and German expressionism. It tells me something about the particular style of inwardness that I find in Butoh. Finally, Butoh cultivated its own form (or forms) of postmodern expressionism. Butoh has variety: it can be understated and nude (Tanaka), antiheroic and wild (Hijikata), spiritual (Ohno), mystical (Amagatsu), existentially dark and void (Ashikawa), or uplifting (Nakajima). Sometimes a single work will contain all of this—as in Kayo Mikami's *Kenka* (1992) (*Consecration of Flowers*).

Butoh has unmistakable links to German dance (as to modern

Toward the end of *Kenka* (*Consecration of Flowers*), Kayo Mikami looks out from under a tent of reeds, and the dancer as shape-shifter con-jures shamanic images. *Photograph by André Chambat.*

dance), but its development gathered up modern dance and recreated it on Japanese grounds. Butoh's modern dance roots, as we briefly explored, were the same as those that influenced the technically ascendant, musically phrased Japanese concert dance. But Butoh went another way. Butoh revived the very heartbeat of modern dance—its downward descent into the body psyche—and it did this by looking into the heart of Japan. We see that Butoh is certainly as close to the slow time and small steps of Noh theater (a classical form of Japanese drama with choral music and dancing) as it is to the more spatially expansive expressionist modern dance. Butoh's unique revival of expressionism recalls Germany and the inventiveness of modern dance, but Butoh also evokes the expressive abstracted content of Japanese Ukiyo-e and the bawdy Kabuki. It was, after all, the influence of the Ukiyo-e woodcuts upon the French impressionist artists in the late nineteenth century that began the West's fascination with Japanese stylization.[19]

The growth of modern dance and ballet in the United States also exhibited a popular fascination with Japan, especially with Ukiyo-e stylization (Graham as she ornaments her upswept knotted hair for Jocasta, for instance).[20] In its early development, modern dance in the United States and Germany thrived on what it deemed Oriental and exotic.[21] Graham and Wigman, even as they turned toward Greek mythology, embraced a Japanese stylistic flair for abstraction. Isamu Noguchi's sets brought Japanese bare bones design to Graham's works, and Wigman's inscrutable Nohlike masks abstracted her frenzied movements. Ernst Scheyer, professor of art history and a reviewer of dance concerts in Germany from 1930 to 1933, watched Wigman's work grow over time. He believes that Greek art in its classical and archaic phases formed the bedrock of Wigman's taste, but he also explores how Wigman's *Witch Dance* (1926) was created under stimulation of Japanese and Javanese art.[22] Wigman's lucid masks, some of which were made by Victor Magito who had worked with Japanese Noh masks, gave her a route from expressionism to abstraction. The masks created what Ernst Scheyer calls a timeless and overwhelming "eerie stillness" amid the wildest leaps.[23]

Butoh circles back and goes underneath modern dance as it rediscovers Ukiyo-e's bold foreshortening, soft-ground etching, high contrast, asymmetry, intimate emotional space, and casual snapshot effect; especially its stylized body movement and expressive facial gestures. Butoh also paces itself in the ghostly timelessness of Noh drama, and its rice-powdered face becomes the universalized mask, as we shall take up. When we examine the East/West amalgamations of Butoh, it becomes increasingly apparent that we should not simply credit the emergence of modern dance to the United States and Germany. Clearly, it arose more globally. Modern dance abstracted, interpreted, and distilled its choreographic essences from sources around the world,[24] and it borrowed extensively from Japanese aesthetics.

In drawing forward the abstract expressionism of modern dance, perhaps Butoh borrowed back what modern dance had already borrowed from Japan. While she saw no direct quotations, New York critic Jennifer Dunning accused Natsu Nakajima of imitating Graham in her performance of *Sleep and Reincarnation*.[25] But who/what was Graham imitating, and how desirable (or possible) is it to be completely original? America is a culture that prizes originality (and the contracted ego), sometimes to the exclusion of tradition and cooperative or communal values. Contemporary Butoh, especially through the work of Akira Kasai and Yumiko Yoshioka, is interested in making an aesthetic case for the body without boundaries, the shared "community body," or descent of the egotistical self (as I explore in the final chapter). In any case, aesthetic and cultural exchange is not a contest, nor a crime. It is research and sharing and one of the ways we have of experiencing the other (even as we know that good research also credits its sources). The spirit of Butoh continues an international interface, and it moves underneath some of the so-called Oriental sources for modern dance as it goes back to pre-Western Japan. Butoh originated as Japanese, but also had roots in the creative individualism, self-interrogation, and abstract expressionism of modern dance. Butoh recreates the ethnic eclecticism of modern dance in its utilization of global sources. Now Butoh and its techniques for revitalizing the body have spread internationally, influencing a spectrum of aesthetic styles in dance, drama, photography, and the visual arts.

As an unforeseen outcome, the therapeutic implications of Butoh are also being explored by Natsu Nakajima, myself, and others such as Toru Iwashita, whom I write about in "Liebe." Nakajima, who introduced me to Butoh, works as a dance therapist as she continues to choreograph and dance. She figures strongly in several of my essays. Through her influence and that

of Kazuo Ohno, I now incorporate Butoh improvisation (or "dancing the dreambody," as I call it) in my workshops and training
programs, bridging dance and somatic therapy. Iwashita continues to dance with Sankai Juku and works as a dance therapist in
a psychiatric hospital while developing a free-form Butoh in solos
like *Houge*, a dance performed in silence.

Supported by folk and spiritual precedent, Butoh is continuing to prove that in a conservative culture like Japan there is room
for experiment and renewal alongside tradition and continuity. In
Japanese aesthetics the historical cultivation of bombast and dis-
tortion exists alongside harmonious understatement and minimalism. This is true of both folk art and traditional (classical)
theater. What is named by critic Masakatsu Gunji "shuaku no
bi" (aesthetics of ugliness) is a legitimate aspect of folk and classical art in Japan's "rituals of inversion," where grotesque antics
are allowed.[26]

Similarly, a patient introversion supports the tolerant inner
dance of Zen where images of all kinds are allowed free play
without repression, and Zen's contained neutrality invites non-
attachment, neither praise nor blame but being (itself). Such simple presence is cultivated in Noh dance (and masks) as a form of
Zen. Noh, I have come to understand, is remote for many Japanese, as it certainly can be for outsiders. I think I was prepared for
Noh partly through my acquaintance with meditation and in a
more curious way through Butoh.

Butoh, Zen, and Japan come together for me. They hold the
fascination of otherness, but I have also made them my own. I rec-

ognize my body/soul in Butoh, and my longing for pure silence and emptying out in the Zen aspect of "one pointedness." Some of my experiences of Butoh have indeed been single-pointed in consciousness, a stream of nows like movement meditations. Such experiences may come through many different means, including walks in nature and purely focused classical dance forms. So it is not my intention to link Butoh and Zen, except where they have intersected in my own experience, and where I recognize that Butoh draws upon Zen as a matter of style, or concept. Butoh derives from the same existential concept of Zen that Shunru Suzuki has called "beginner's mind," and it also develops a Zen-like emptiness (called *mu*) that invites the irrational moment of sudden self-remembering and spontaneous renewal.

Forgotten Garden

The Garden of Life
(Willows are green
and flowers red)

September 18, 1985

Natsu Nakajima's dance *Niwa (The Garden)* was performed for the first time in North America at the Festival of New Dance in Montreal in September 1985. I knew nothing about Butoh then and was completely surprised by the effect it had on me. Through the late nineteen sixties and seventies, I had become so accustomed to American dance and its objective attitude toward performance that I was moved more than ever by the unabashed honest emotion expressed in Nakajima's Butoh. I experienced its truth as my own. The dance was not objectively calculated; it sprang from subjective, felt life, as Butoh attempts to shed the body of social habits. I couldn't help thinking back to the raw beginnings of modern dance, and what it must have been like to see Isadora Duncan dance, or Mary Wigman. Similar psychological probings are apparent in Nakajima's dance. Moreover, like Duncan and Wigman, Nakajima has the ability to draw the audience into her emotional vortex, opening them to their own inner dance.

Niwa is a full evening's work. Nakajima explains that "Niwa is a forgotten garden, very small and very Japanese, the garden of my memory, my childhood. . . . I created this work to see my own life, placing myself as a woman, sitting in the garden, looking at it grow old and fade away." Nakajima performs Niwa with a partner, Yuriko Maezawa, becoming her double to allow for magical disappearances and emergences with instant changes of costumes. Except for one short duet, the dance is performed by the two of them as a long solo, as they change places imperceptibly in short blackouts. The difference between "the two" disappears into "the one." Together they present a single journey, from birth to enlightenment.

Niwa takes us on a journey through our inner life, communicated primarily through the dancers' facial expressions, as the soul is reflected in them. The gestures of hands and arms, however large or slight, are deeply etched in space, and often washed in blazing light. The face is painted white, creating an anti-individualistic effect. The dancing face is the face of everyone. It assumes the aspect of a lucid mask, through which we are allowed to see our own face and to feel the fluctuation of our emotions. In *Niwa*, we view our innermost secret face—of hope and disgust, of anguish, laughter, and serenity.

Each section is complete, but relative to the whole, like panels on a folding screen. In the beginning of the dance, Nakajima's outline materializes out of darkness, seeming transparent in the white and gathering light. She appears wrapped in a simple drape, holding sheaves of dried reeds or flowers in front of her and just overhead. The bundle draws her forward, as her body inclines slightly away from the line of movement. Her holding back creates internal tension, as she inches ahead ever so slowly, foot by foot, into blinding light. A look of ecstasy and wonder spreads on her masklike face, creased by the celestial sounds of the music. Her endlessly slow sojourn is enveloped in widening pools of repeated sound as the music gathers shattering strength, then fades to nothing. This is the first full image in the work, the section she calls "Nanakusa," "Seven Grasses," an image of childhood recollections that breaks suddenly and darkens at its apex.

She has traveled from the upstage left third of the space, that most powerful *jo* place for slow beginnings in Noh theater. She stops in the center, or *ha*, the climactic spot that opens a new beginning. This will lead toward ever contracting and expanding cycles, typical of Japanese theater, culminating in a dramatic release called *kyu*. This cyclic aesthetic of *Jo-ha-kyu*, at the heart of classical Japanese theater, is also at the heart of much Butoh, especially *Niwa*.[1]

The constantly assembling *jo* image is finally intensified in white-hot light, then suddenly cut away at center stage. After a long and trembling growth, it continues to vibrate for a moment in the darkness—or glow in the mind. In the next instant, we see "The Infant," a new image of the same female figure, now huddled under a small tentlike cover with only her head and face emerging. As her head peeks out, it seems to get pulled back inside. It emerges through struggle, the facial expressions integrating and disintegrating oddly over time. Just so, poeticized images from grotesque to beautiful develop throughout. Or rather, shades of emotion are released and flow together as layers of feeling are explored in vivid dreamtime.

Nakajima explores stages of life common to all. She recalls primal instincts in "The Infant," but within a personal vision. She sucks and holds on. Her terror of evacuation from Sakhalin Island as a baby is remembered and powerfully distilled in this section. Out of this, "The Dream" appears, as the innocence of girlhood is cherished in shimmering movement, light, and sound. The dream is laced with nightmares and humor. Nakajima and Maezawa dance a duet of two grinning insects. This image gives way to mature womanhood and memories of love in "Masks & Black Hair." Here Nakajima displays a womanly warmth and wit stereotypically Japanese in small gestures of the shoulders and tilts of the face. She plays on a wobbly walk with arms loosely flung, then ardently drawn back into place.

In the next transformation of costume and mood, "The Ghost" appears, bringing regret and loss, loss of power as the gestures

Natsu Nakajima, one of the female founders of Butoh, in "The Infant," a section of her dance *Niwa* (The Garden). She hears muffled gunfire and a foghorn in the distance as she is evacuated from Sakhalin Island as an infant, thus the name of her dance company Mutiki Sha (Fog Horn). *Photograph by Nourit Masson Sekine.*

weaken, and loss of human features as a dull mask takes the place of the dancer's once-white face. Sitting on the floor, the ghost nods her head and shakes her hands. Her head doesn't seem to know what her hands are doing. There are intimations of insanity. She turns away to erase the gaze of the audience. When her face appears again, the muddy mask has turned a burnished red. Supernaturally, she has turned it around in a instant. Her hands clasp together with restraint toward the end of "The Ghost" section, then open slowly. The finger points, but the arm drops away from

Natsu Nakajima in "The Ghost" section of her dance *Niwa*. Here she lifts up from the floor and signals from a crouch before returning to the floor in her mud mask—its gray color turning to red as it is deftly manipulated while her face is buried in her hands. *Photograph by Nourit Masson-Sekine.*

it in sudden shock. The ghost disappears, and "Kannon" rises in its place. This is the pure world of containment that Nakajima calls "World of innocence, stillness—fluent energy of eternity." In this world, her body is transfigured and robed in gold.

In "Kannon," Nakajima moves up from a kneeling position in graceful inclines, finally arriving at a fully centered stance, opening the splendor of the music to us, as her face turns to meet our gaze. Human suffering is being born across a sea of darkness by the compassionate Bodhisattva Kannon. Over time, her face releases in detached rapture (kyu) as the Bailero from *Songs of the Auvergne* evokes the religious sublime. The dancer's facial transfigurations conjure Goddess icons: the burning Kali (Hindu), the wise and awesome Tara (Buddhist), and the mysterious Madonna (Christian). As the lights fade out, the glowing dancer links the tip of her thumb and first finger in a timeless Buddhist *mudra*, the only literal symbol in the work. Kannon, the Goddess of mercy, is Kwan-Yin in China. She also has origins as a God in India. Metamorphosis is an aspect of her power, thus her sex is uncertain. She/he has been said to appear in whatever form is needed.

Butoh scholar Susan Klein notices that *Niwa* derives from premodern Japanese religious life both Shinto and Buddhist. As the dance aims to bring the body into mystical union with nature, it bears a relationship to Zen Buddhism in particular.[2] This is explicit in Nakajima's use of the garden as symbol of her life. In Zen gardens, life cycles and world as cosmos may be contemplated.

As the dancers take their bows, they celebrate the Asian sources of the work with undulating torsos, twining arm gestures, and punctuated hand mudras. Finally, a formal Japanese kneeling bow lowering the head to the floor pays deepest respect to the audience, making them one with the dance.

Even though Nakajima's Butoh lays no claim to Western modern dance, there are, nevertheless, important similarities. It grows out of the same search for the primal instinctual self that motivated the beginnings of Western modern dance. "The Ghost" in *Niwa* indeed summons up Mary Wigman's grotesque *Witch Dance* with the same spirit, which admits the dark reaches of the psyche in dances more expressive than technical, more starkly gestured than flowing. (I made this comparison with Wigman in my first article on *Niwa*, presented at an aesthetics conference for the Canadian Society for aesthetics in 1985. Later I learned that critic Marcia Seigel had made a similar comparison in her review, "Flickering Stones,"[3] and that Klein also saw the resemblance to Wigman.[4])

In its dark diaphanous nature, Butoh, like the original modern dance, takes its essence from our feminine (yin) body, the dark symbol of myth, our earth body, or the Great Goddess archetype. This is the mythic symbol that Joseph Campbell has described in his books and seminars as "nonjudgmental" and "transparent," the "yielding" (yin) that allows us to pass through that we may come back at ourselves. This is the same universalized feminine that Donna Wilshire poetizes in her writing and singing of hymns to the Triple Goddess: *Virgin, Mother, Crone.*[5]

Nakajima's work is clearly in the stream of female innovators Isadora Duncan, Ruth St. Denis, Mary Wigman, Doris Humphrey, and Martha Graham, who founded twentieth-century modern dance and aided the return of the Great Goddess in the consciousness of our time. This stream has now become a river. Each dancer in her own way sought to unearth the wisdom of the primal body hidden beneath cultural manners. St. Denis sounded out the mysterious body, Wigman the demonic and emotional, Humphrey the body of physical law, and Graham worked with her belief in the body that "never lies."

Like Duncan, in particular, Nakajima has sought to liberate

the natural body and its highest truths. For her, as for Duncan, art is a means and not an end. This is readily apparent in *Niwa*, and clearly stated by Nakajima.

"I am striving," she says, "not towards art, but towards love."

I went to visit Natsu in Japan a year after seeing her dance. I was eager to meet her and had been knitting a scarf as a present. I wanted to make something with my own hands for the bringer of *Niwa*. As we spoke on the phone in Tokyo, she said she would meet me in front of "Armands." I asked if it was a French restaurant. She said no, I would see when I got there. We were having some trouble communicating.

She asked how she would know me?

I said, "I'll be with a tall American man."

She replied, "Well, all the foreigners are tall."

This didn't seem to help.

So I asked, "How will I know you?"

She said, "I'll be short, and I have a long black ponytail."

I just took a deep breath, and said to myself—

"Well, I'll find her."

When I came up out of the subway, I was facing a candy store called "Almonds," and every other person had a long black ponytail. I stood for a moment, and turned slowly surveying the crowd. There she was; it must be—the composure, the antiheroic feminine sublime I had seen in her face at the end of *Niwa*, as she transformed from the Ghost to the Goddess. With no makeup, and no lighting effects, the poetics of her person were still evident. She was not demurring, obviously independent, yet fully receptive.

I gave her the scarf that evening at dinner. She joked about her inability to make ends meet as a Butoh artist and said maybe she should take up that most secure position in Japan of "housewife." My acquaintance with Natsu began my Butoh odyssey. She took me to meet Kazuo Ohno in Yokohama and eventually came to Brockport to teach my students. She could communicate to Western students and eventually choreographed for a group she assembled in New York to perform *Sleep and Reincarnation*, at La Mama. My student Valerie Talbot went to dance with her. Valerie, who had both dance and acting experience, said it was the most demanding performance she had ever been involved in. This was not anything-goes improvisation. (There is a mistaken notion that all Butoh is essentially improvised in performance.)[6] It was very exacting choreography, down to the last eye blink. Natsu was a taskmaster. She knew the tasks, and had them mastered.

The Marble Bath

Ryokan
in
Takayama

照一
隅燈

Light of
a Stone Lantern
(A lantern
lights
the corner)

August 21, 1986

Alone in the marble bath,
she danced

Like jewels, drops of water
glistened on her breasts

Her image reflected from the
sunlight on the wet floor,
in the mirror and in the
window, woven with the
garden beyond it

The stone lantern flickered
as the sun faded
in the garden,
on the marble
in the mirror,
the window,
the image.

My

Mother

Mother Goddess
(Kind-Mother
Kwan-Yin,
the female Buddha)

I carry all the dead with me.

Kazuo Ohno

August 17, 1986

Kazuo Ohno was an old man in his eighties when I watched him teach a Butoh class in Yokohama, Japan, on a hot summer evening in a small studio beside his house. I was struck more than anything else by the qualities and meaning of the mother goddess in his teaching and the feminine sensitivity of his impromptu performance after class of a part of his famous dance called *My Mother*, a delicate dance made more poignant by Ohno's age. *My Mother* goes to the heart of Butoh, the dance of darkness, that originated with Ohno and his partner Tatsumi Hijikata.

The dark feminine principle, subconscious spontaneous life, is the main metaphor for Butoh, its aesthetic core. Like eruptions from the subconscious, Butoh performances can take any shape. They may shock and surprise, edify and enlighten, disgust or delight. It is not surprising that Butoh draws from a paradigm of the feminine. Traditional Japanese arts are pervaded with a sensitive stylized feminine, and the principle mythic deity of Japan is the Great Sun Goddess, Omikami Amaterasu.

It is significant to Butoh and to Ohno's work that the feminine and masculine often blur in Japan. Way back in stories of Japan's beginnings, the Great Goddess, Amaterasu, dressed up in male clothes when she met her disobedient brother, Susano-o. Gender bending such as Ohno's is in tune with Japanese myth and theater. Of practical note is the fact that the national dress, the kimono, is worn by both sexes. Men typically perform female roles in Japanese theater. The Japanese like to say, "When a woman is feminine, that's nature, but when a man can show us the feminine on stage, that's art."

It is no surprise either that Butoh is mystical in essence, that it often moves with the eternally slow, internally tuned rhythms of Noh theater (akin to the slow rhythm of the earth and devoted patience of the goddess mother). It rejects the post-West refinements of traditional Japanese theater such as Noh and Kabuki in

order to go back (or forward) to unstudied spontaneous movement. At the same time, it employs basic elements of Noh and
Kabuki, reflective of premodern Japanese aesthetics. *Butoh often
seems to float,* like Noh theater (and Ukiyo-e, "Pictures of the Floating World School," discussed in the introduction). I saw Noh
theater for the first time in Tokyo the night before my visit to
Ohno's studio. To me, Noh is like an elaborate extended chant,
or a floating tone poem, combining music, movement, story, and
costumes in a polished sparse setting. In Noh, drums and a flute
in tandem with voices provide exquisitely simple music, matched
by minimal restrained gestures, movement, and masks of contrasting qualities—one serene, the other sinister. Deliberate minute
steps and once in a while a single stamp of the foot combine with
unexpected drum accents and the slowest possible turning of the
figure in space. Like Noh, Butoh stretches both time and space.
Noh is highly formalized and ritualistic, however, while Butoh
is expressionistic, growing from individual experience and creativity.

I was introduced to Butoh in 1985 by Natsu Nakajima through
her mesmerizing solo, *Niwa (The Garden).* As a result, I corre-
sponded with her, and met her in Tokyo. Now she was taking me
to meet Ohno in Yokohama. Nakajima had studied and danced
with Ohno and Hijikata during Butoh's early experiments. She
didn't have money to pay for her classes with Ohno, she told me;
so Ohno paid her train fare to his studio. Subsequently, Nakajima
became an important female founder of the Butoh aesthetic.

This balmy August evening, Nakajima and I took the train from

The author's snapshot of a workshop class at Kazuo Ohno's studio in Yokohama. Students listen to Ohno introduce the theme before beginning to improvise while the translator Akiko Akane (with pen in hand) sits next to Ohno.

Tokyo, then walked to Ohno's studio high up on a hill along a winding path. Before class started, Ohno showed me pictures and posters of his performances. It was amazing that he was still contemplating a full schedule of performances, worldwide, at eighty. But, as I observed, in dance not limited to athleticism and youth, this is not only possible, but desirable.

The studio was more like a large living room, much like my memories of the small homey Wigman studio in Berlin, not at all reminiscent of institutional studios I had become used to. The class began with students gathering around Ohno. He spoke to them for about half an hour before they began to move. That night's theme concerned the human dance inside the womb. "I learned Butoh," Ohno said, "inside my mother's womb. . . . All dancing and all of the arts come from this source."

He continued to explain that when a sperm unites with an egg, it lives; but many others die, just as in the world many people and their deaths contribute to one life. Thus the personality is complex; it has many layers from all that has affected it. He went on to point out that all life is fragile and should be protected, not only one's own life, but that of others as well. He linked all this to the erotic and to the mother, saying that we, as human beings, are erotic in our very nature and life, since the erotic is close to the origins of life. A man and woman unite to bring forth life. Eventually we are born and separate from the mother, but our original bond with her contains the erotic union of the mother and the father. (His way of inspiring students to improvise by developing an idea or image also relates to Wigman's teaching method, as discussed in the introduction.)

Just before the students were to begin the improvisation, Ohno stood up and told them to remember the dance inside their mother's womb, not to think about it, but to move from "the feeling of it." He stressed the "perfect freedom" of the fetus, a point he developed further after the improvisation began. The content of the dance, he said, should not be important. "Do not think, what shall I do? Move randomly out of intuition." To illustrate his meaning, Ohno suddenly grasped a letter nearby, and held it up rashly. "I do not need to look inside the letter to see what is there. If I have perfect freedom, I can do anything with it. Instead of reading the letter, I can eat it." He then bit into the letter, evoking spontaneous laughter from the students, breaking their mood of rapt attention, encouraging abandon.

Each person took a place in the small intimate space of the studio and began to move. Each one had an individual presence, yet all moved with a peaceful innocence. No one moved far from the spot they had chosen. The dancer's movements were soft, sensitively detailed with subtle movement of hands, head, legs, and feet. Often their eyes were closed to tune their movements more closely to the inner dance of the womb. Much of the dance could not be seen. It was on the inside, sometimes more imagined than done. Once Ohno stopped them, very briefly, to say that the fetus moves toward freedom. "It always wants something more in its incompleteness," he said. The dancers began to enlarge their space with minute strivings and longings.

Still the movement remained delicate and introspective, except for occasional bursts, jabs, and thrusts. This was not so much the body talking as it was listening, seeking to hear where the next movement should go. Ohno was playing soft Japanese harp music in the background. The total vision of the dance and music together evoked a floating, soft, and blissful world, punctuated with a bewilderment of obstacles overcome in the gradual unfolding of the whole.

After class, Ohno performed a portion of his solo *My Mother* for us, and had fresh plums, glistening with chilled water, brought from his home next door. The movements of his dance recalled the class improvisation, and took on even more meaning for me, because of his discussions of the mother as our original connection with the erotic and growth toward freedom. "I do not agree with those who dance without emotion," he told me later. He said he disliked most Western dance, because "it is too intellectual and too violent." Dance should be "innocence and intoxication."

On the way back to Tokyo, I asked Nakajima what Ohno might have been saying to students as he occasionally spoke to them individually, almost in a whisper during the improvisation, giving them suggestions. She said that whatever they were doing, he would tell them to do the opposite.

Nakajima was familiar with this teaching technique, and it made sense to me in view of Ohno's irrational bite out of the letter. It is important in dance (and life) to sometimes disrupt habitual flow, in order to free the self. It is not easy to free instinctual movement, to be spontaneous. Habit is ingrained. Even skill may fall inside habit's orbit, depending on consciousness and intent. Merce Cunningham used "chance" in his choreography to "get away from himself," as he explained in his classes. Ohno encourages his students to let their movement be, yet not to be satisfied with it.

Ohno provokes a tender restraint of the voluntary nervous system. This allows the involuntary to manifest its subtle wisdom, as takes place in the relaxation response and in meditation. Like a somatic therapist, Ohno encourages a clearing of the body's habits to stimulate new freedoms. There is in his style a bodily lived self-effacement unique to Butoh, however. It challenges culture's violence toward the body, recognizing "the body that has been robbed," as Butoh calls it. Butoh seeks organic instinctual movement. It is nature's body and our own nature that Butoh seeks to restore. This is why Min Tanaka and others have made use of natural environments and nudity, and Butoh has sometimes favored communal living close to nature.

Yet, it is obvious that Butoh is itself a cultural expression. It sets up a dialectic between the natural and the cultural. Ohno works through a gentle amelioration of the cultural body, to free the innocent body. He then instantiates this body in highly stylized Butoh theater. Underneath the paint and costumes, however, Ohno's style is somatically sound. He teaches a conscious awareness through movement that Moshe Feldenkrais might well have appreciated. His emphasis on the means whereby a movement is accomplished, rather than the results, would have pleased F. M. Alexander. In contrast, Hijikata's style prompted a more violent overthrow or gestalt transplant of "the missing body." Good improvisation and good performances are edged with what is missing, what is not there by omission, intimations of what might be, as well as what is. In Yokohama, Ohno's spontaneous solo performance of *My Mother* called forth the maternal in both the presence and the absence of his mother. However absent materially, she was real in Ohno's gestures. They issued from a listening body, well attuned and waiting.

Shibui
and
the
Sublime

*Sankai
Juku's
Performance
in
Montreal*

We found in our mind a *superiority over nature* itself in its immensity. In the same way, though the irresistibility of nature's might makes us, considered as natural beings, recognize our physical impotence, it reveals in us at the same time an ability to judge ourselves independent of nature, and reveals in us a *superiority over nature* that is the basis of a self-preservation quite different in kind.

> *Emmanuel Kant on "The Sublime,"*
> Critique of Judgment (*my emphasis*)

Meeting of
Birth and Death
(Life and death
are the same)

Introduction, May 12, 1996

When I asked my friend Midori Sato who teaches dance at Budo International University in Japan if she could see *shibui* in the Butoh aesthetic of Sankai Juku dance company, she said, "yes," without hesitation. Then we nodded our heads in the affirmative and repeated the Japanese term—*shibui*. Immediately we thought of a friend whose good taste in dress and unimposing character we found natural and at the same time striking: *shibui*.

There is something more our friend has in common with Sankai Juku. She also can light up a room or a space in the mind. With Sankai Juku this happens through dance, lighting design, and staged architecture. With her it is a matter of personality. Her quiet smile is sublime. Moreover, it is a part of her nature. One might argue that her smile is merely beautiful; but that would be too decorative a term to describe its mesmerizing effect.

My friend's smile and the aesthetic of Sankai Juku has led me to question the Kantian sublime (as quoted above). Sankai Juku unfolds a sublime in blissful harmony with nature, although far more theatrical than my friend's smile. Stylistically, I associate the company's dancing with the Japanese term, *shibui*, an aesthetic subtlety that requires further explanation. In locating the Sankai Juku historically, I also examine its relationship to German expressionism, past and present.

I contrast Sankai Juku's aesthetic with the sexually conflicted sublime of German expressionist Pina Bausch. The romantic sublimity of classical ballet in its overcoming of nature (gravity and the flesh) provides yet another contrast. The sublime of Western aesthetics has its source in Kant and is achieved at the expense of nature.

The mind's struggle for superiority over nature is brilliantly outlined by Kant in admitting his own terror of impotence in the face of nature's immensity and power. Nature is nothing to be joined for Kant. Yet he sees that we are "natural beings." He looks out on nature and separates himself. His contemplation is given to a supposed superiority of the mind over nature, not a mind that is a part of nature.

Is there a way out of this dualistic sublime? I think so. When I see the ocean, there is awe in me; I also want to get in and swim. Not separating myself from the scene or the water, the water logic of my mind wants to join the ocean to the watery essence of myself. In a similar way, I join the watery essence of Sankai Juku.

A product of Ushio Amagatsu's choreography, the Sankai Juku Butoh company is a captivating hybrid of late twentieth century international developments in theater, dance, and stage design. It had its genesis in Japan but was for many years located in Paris. Like German choreographer Pina Bausch, Amagatsu blurs the lines between dance and theater. Like Bausch, he is also a revolutionary figure in establishing a popular level of dance theater that is nevertheless esoteric (and violent).

Sankai Juku's emotional spectrum evolves from a luminous ground, a coming into being of theatrical elements with human embodiment. Often creaturelike, the eerie dancer-beings pass through sublime moments of self-emergence, with only intimations of distinct personality and individuality. Human form is wrought through expansive/contractive movement development, divinely suspended in mythical time. When violence erupts, it seems to come from nowhere, suddenly moving through the dancers like earthquakes and inner storms.

Inheritors of Expressionism

The agony in Amagatsu's work is not stated through willful struggles for dominion, unlike the abrasive gender clashes in the Tanztheater of Bausch. Yet we could rightly call both Amagatsu and Bausch revivals of early twentieth century expressionism as it appeared in the bleak dances and gaunt masks of Mary Wigman (as mentioned in the introduction), the tightly drawn dramas of Kurt Jooss, and the bald majesty of Harald Kreutzberg. The morbidity and moodiness of the 1890s lay in the background. Here James Ensor's paintings of grotesque masks (*Intrigue*, 1890) come to mind. As harbinger of dance expressionism, some of Wigman's first themes included dances of death, and poetry of the Orient. The 1926 version of *Witch Dance* sprang from features of Javanese and Japanese cultures. "In it the demonic and animal instincts were controlled by a severe dance style."[1]

Expressionism (a wide and imprecise term) was fermenting at the turn of the twentieth century. It was preceded by the poetic ecstasies of Nietzsche's antiphilosophy in the West, and in Japan by the sharp pain, sensuous indulgence, and controlled frenzy arising in Ukiyo-e woodcuts of the seventeenth century. This art excelled in depicting the human figure in boldly abstract flowing motion and lasted into the nineteenth century (as discussed in the introduction). Ukiyo-e's eloquent style still speaks to something essentially Japanese with its genius for synthesis and lean design. As pure design it is perhaps unrivaled.[2] Its emotional subject matter and lean abstraction preceded twentieth-century expressionism in all of the arts. Its suave flowing style, however, makes it difficult to reconcile with the bleakness of European expressionism. This is also true of Sankai Juku.

European expressionism came on the heels of Fauvism, full of wild color and distortions. A clear example is the work of French painter Georges Rouault, especially his bleeding and passionate *Head of Christ*, 1905. The Fauves (the wild beasts) influenced Die Brucke (The Bridge), a group of painters living in Dresden in 1905 who explored emotional styles, including Ernst Kirchner (*Street*, 1907) and Emil Nolde. In 1912, the year that he met Wigman, Nolde painted his *Candle Dancers* in bold reds, purples, and yellows. After the First World War, he painted his famous portrait of Wigman in watercolor on Japanese paper (1923).

Choreographer Oskar Schlemmer (1888–1943), although abstract and architectural, drew upon the early twentieth century's concern for primeval direct expression in his *gesamtkunstwerk* (total work of art) integrating theater, graphic art, dance, and stage design. His search for an absolute mathematics in his *Triadic Ballet* (1922) placed him closer to classical forms, distinguishing his work from the visceral intuitive, dark vitality of European expressionism.

Both Bausch and Amagatsu are the heirs of expressionism and

the total theater concepts of *gesamtkunstwerk*, but their differences are marked. Bausch is psychologically dark and overtly dramatic. *Murderer, Hope of Women* (1907), the revolutionary play of Oskar Kokoschka, anticipates Bausch's preoccupation with the brutalized feminine. In contrast, Amagatsu is inward, spiritual, and mystical, but he retains an expressionist intention. Like expressionism as it finally filled galleries and performance halls by 1924, Amagatsu has abstracted (drawn away from) his subject, while producing an individually inspired spiritual vision of the raw materials of emotional life. What distinguishes Amagatsu's work from European expressionism, however, is its delicate restraint (its *shibui*) and the distinctly Eastern way in which nature is treated.

Power and Violence

From earliest times, the Japanese have based their arts in an unpretentious devotion to nature. Literature and legend bear the imprint of landscape. Painting and textiles all demonstrate the love of flowers and trees, birds and animals. Poems extol Fuji, the peerless mountain, and Lake Biwa. Birds and insects are revered as subjects for representation but are abstracted in striking lines and economical strokes. Harunobu and Koryusai, Utamaro, and Hokusai all excelled in this, producing exquisite designs of flowers, birds, and animals that order and pattern nature without destroying its vitality.[3]

Nature is also Amagatsu's theme as he paints whole landscapes of motion—not in the representational fashion of Ukiyo-e, however, but still within Ukiyo-e's appreciation for material nature and the expressive body. Amagatsu's aesthetic of the body drops beneath personalized surfaces as he seeks to bring our hidden (human) nature to the surface. He probes the primordial undercurrent of the given expressiveness of the body. In *Jomon Sho (Homage to Prehistory)*, he is called home to bodily origins and intrinsic expression. His preoccupation with the primordial body is related to a collective unconscious, as has been a Butoh concern.[4]

Amagatsu amplifies our body's kinship with animals, birds, fish, and insects. Once he danced with a live peacock on his back, the regal bird glowing purple-blue and green against his powdered white and shaven body. His ability to stage such events and to magnify the proportions of envisioned nature place his work within the auspices of *the sublime*, aesthetically characterized by its power to overwhelm the senses. Consider, for instance, the vastness of the sea and sky (incomprehensible in space). Imagine eternity (unimaginable time itself).

Amagatsu catches us off guard with his mystical vision: his boundless flow and temporal displacement. Most of all it is time (as poured through human emergence) that founds the sublime in Amagatsu's work. Phenomenal and eternal time are sublimely woven together in Amagatsu's dances for Sankai Juku. Nature (time and the body's evolution) is thematized, not suppressed or dominated as in Western dualistic expressions of the sublime. The sublime the West incorporated from Immanuel Kant's theory of aesthetic measure was based on disinterested judgments elevating pure reason above nature, releasing the self's instinct for power. Dualistic aesthetics wrought through the friction of two fundamentally opposed extremes is in fact founded on the Kantian sublime that Thomas Huhn calls *"a nostalgia for Violence."*[5]

This is the violence that divides us from nature. It fears nature, feeling impotent in the face of its immensity and might. Kant's sublime (as we saw at the beginning) involves the terror of masculine impotence and thus provokes a negation of nature. Power lies in the mind's control over nature. This is the very nature that is so wedded to the mythical mother earth, the dark feminine paradigm that has symbolized nature. Awe is mixed with terror in the masculine/romantic Kantian sublime. The mind's struggle with nature's powers and our ability "to judge ourselves independent of nature" is the basis for transcendent feelings of overcoming; the power of the mind is pitted against "the irresistibility of nature's might."[6]

In the Kantian sublime there is no "intuited accord between the self and the world, but only the noumenal power of the self," as Maire Kurrik explains in *Literature and Negation.*[7] The mind's superiority and our heightened feeling is bought at the cost of our consonance with the world and devotion to the earth. Such a sublime is based on a disjunction with organic nature and the organically generative nature of our body, also. It depends on the typical turbulence and pathos we have come to associate with the heightened mind of male sublimity. As Hume explains: "'Difficulty,' does not dampen the mind's alacrity. Instead, it has the contrary effect, of sustaining and increasing it."[8]

This is especially evident in dances that seek to overcome nature rather than to acknowledge or incorporate it. But, we might well ask, "what does nature refer to in dance"? Nature in dance might refer us to the nature of the body, as I shall take up. Or it could point in the direction of our gendered reality in terms of body—an aspect of both nature and culture.

The Terrible Sublime of Pina Bausch

Dancing bodies are not genderless, although the dancers of Sankai Juku come close to creating a neutral sex, with their shaven heads like that of celibate nuns and Buddhist priests. Their whitened bodies also mask gender. In a 1984 review, N. Hara suggests that Sankai Juku's dancers are genderless beings: "The lean, naked figures on stage look more like hairless, mutant cats." Male/female binary pairs never occur in Amagatsu's choreography, nor is conflict set up between human antagonists. So the aesthetic tension must be built from another basis.

In contrast, there are acute gender problematics in the agnostic dances of Pina Bausch. This is apparent in such dances as *Rites of Spring*, *Cafe Muller*, *Bluebeard*, and *Kontakthof*. They revolve around gender differences, as they escalate male/female divisions in conflict. Bausch's dances are big and bold. They are staged extravaganzas of overcoming, important statements of strife between the sexes and within the self. They certainly do not turn away from gender dualism or cultural violence. They want to display it, but for a larger purpose (I believe) than mere display.

There seems in Bausch no natural resolution for sexual tension.

This would be the "gender trouble" that philosopher-linguist Judith Butler has identified.[9] The harmonious beauty that provides the aesthetic basis for male/female complementary partnering in classical ballet cannot be found in Bausch. The thrall of her works summons a terrible sublime. Her aesthetic is not beautiful, nor does it produce the pleasure we associate with this term. She exploits the terror of male impotence in the face of feminine sexuality and plays upon cruelty in both sexes. The virgin's blood sacrifice, her dualistic awakening and resistance, is epitomized in Bausch's riveting choreography on Stravinsky's *Le Sacre du Printemps* (*The Rites of Spring*, 1975).

There is near loss of breath as the virgin dances to her death. Josephine Endicott, who danced this role for several years, told me in a 1985 interview: "I really dance in *Sacre*, I dance until I die." Bausch's dance grabs and shakes us. There is a psychological mounting and surmounting of energies, but no sublime overcoming of the body by the mind. There is fate, and there is nature's powerful approach. Spring pulses in the blood. The timpani builds to a breaking point, as the dancer pitches forward. She plunges face down like a piece of timber in the silent air. No one stirs after her fall.

In a most telling manner, Bausch leaves us at an existential point, not one of romantic sublimity. She leaves us stranded in the split and turmoil of our sexual dualisms, the death of the virgin, and a bursting of winter's bonds. The virgin is no willing victim in this dance; she dies amid the alienating stares and shoves of the clan as they withdraw.

Pina Baush's neo-expressionist *Rites of Spring* (1975). Near the end
of the dance, the soloist pauses and grips herself in agony before
throwing her body into the fits and clutchings of the final scene.
As harbinger to her dance of death, the group looks on coldly
and without solace. *Photograph by Gert Weigelt.*

Overcoming the Flesh in Ballet

An entirely different kind of dualistic violence is demonstrated in Western dance idioms that are based on the overcoming of material and corporeal nature. Such is the overcoming of gravity, the taming and sublimation of the body we idealize in the classical ballet's mathematical refinement of body postures (the anti-organic ballet vocabulary that feminist Isadora Duncan rejected) and its history of grand spectacle.

The beauty of ballet perfects a cultural body of knowledge based on conformance of the body to linear geometric form. If the ballerina is a flower, she is a well-cultivated one, pure in line. She will fit a form. She is slim in the extreme, and denies her breasts and fleshiness. She menstruates late, or often not at all. Such is the contemporary ballerina in the technocratic twentieth century, but not the more robust ballet figure of the nineteenth. Then the flesh was more accepted, but nevertheless assiduously trained in the ballet's aristocratic social manners. The nineteenth century romantic ballerinas were courtesans, the prized property of men.

The important innovator of ballet in the twentieth century, George Balanchine, is also an owner and cultivator of feminine grace in ballet. "Ballet is a garden of beautiful women, and I am the gardener," he was fond of saying. His gardening is apparent in relation to feminine malleability, a paring down of nature to its (her) very bones. For Balanchine, ballet is above all, "woman." He dedicated his art to her, and married his prima ballerinas. His ballerinas were (and still are) tall and thin. This body type and

Balanchine's unique technical training came to identify *Balanchine's ballerinas*, his creation and possession. His art embodies the Russian classical tradition inherited from Petipa, and ballet's romantic premise of the unattainable ethereal female. His ballerinas are strong, however, never weaklings; but as in all ballet, the movement itself is attuned to breaking the physical bonds of earth's gravity. Balanchine's ballerinas are swift and sure, thus all the more unattainable, sublimely so.

In dance that strives to move beyond the physical, what Oskar Schlemmer acknowledged in his danced architecture as "the bondage of the physical,"[10] the body is the vehicle for the sublime, but only as it is surpassed. Thus the sublime signals a triumph of reason, or mind over body—a mind that is more than merely mental, one that takes pleasure in both concealing and elevating its power over nature. Mind over matter (matter means mother) can also translate as male over female, intellect over body, given these mythological masculine and feminine designations.

The bodily undergoing of the sublime in dualistic aesthetics also employs mind over matter. Kantian aesthetics (the very root of Western aesthetics) explains and generates a subtle violence, manifest in the sublime that Huhn calls a staging of domination as disinterested pleasure.[11] *Disinterested pleasure* is the chilly term that has come to explain "the aesthetic attitude" in Western aesthetic discourse.

But the flesh, by nature, is warm. Thick with the elements of water and earth, the flesh resists its overcoming, and in so doing is not disinterested. Flesh is the interested party, involved in its own duration, not its disappearance. However, as resistance to be overcome (sublimated), flesh is subjected to a transfiguring power. It is willed to a higher aesthetic (or moral) plane, to be purified, transcended.

The flesh is not to be bypassed in any case. It is altogether necessary, as flesh, heavy with breast and buttocks in the dualistic sublime. The flesh-and-blood body *must* participate in superhuman surpassings of its own lived matter (this *is* sublimation), or where is God and the glory? There has to be tension and a foe. Flesh becomes other—the enemy. Unlike the Nigerian dancer in the vital glow of her flesh, called *wanger*,[12] the ballet dancer becomes the enemy of her natural body. The body, the issue and comfort of the mother, is denied. Pathos is realized, and body transcended. This is how the motivating power of "the romantic sublime" achieves the denial of the pleasures of the (mother's) body.[13] Transcendence and denial of the pleasures and powers of the living body go hand in hand in romantic sublimity, for the dancer and also for the audience. Romantic sublimity as it distances the observer's gaze renders the object of his attention all the more attractive. Denial of pleasure whets his desire.

Three Kinds of Sublimity

In Bausch, the social/sexual overcoming (sublimating) of the feminine (flesh) is explored and critiqued. Flesh is not necessarily the enemy, it is owned and suffered. Woman (in Bausch's work) is the flesh. She is the docile and vulgar, abused and avaricious, tensile resister. *She suffers the sublime,* or at least its processes, remaining existentially in her abused flesh and at odds with it. Socialized gender, shame, and self-punishment provide the problematic in Bausch's approach to flesh and the terrible sublime.

In ballet, the subliminal limit is also physical nature in the form of woman's flesh and body, but in an entirely different way than Bausch. Ballet adds flesh to earth's gravity, as it attempts to purify the flesh (to sublimate sexuality) and raise the body above the earth in pointe shoes. Ballet extends this sublimation through airborne lifting of the female by her male partner, etherealizing sensuous pleasure. If she had strings, she would continue heavenward. This is her destination. Such is the disinterested or distanced pleasure of the classical ballet and sublimated formalist dances that quicken the flesh and the bones.

Bausch's orgiastic works are earth offerings. Ballet offers the body up to the air. The Sankai Juku reveals the sublime through the creative (creature) underside of human emergence: gestation and growth, decay and regeneration—as a part of nature. Nature cannot be the villain or the hero, because it offers no real contrast to our humanity. It is our home, our kinship with all life, a dwelling in darkness and light. It is that chain of life that endures, even through transformational change and spontaneous destruction. Containing all colors and possibility, nature is as varied and complex as multicolored human emotions.

Darkness in nature is not necessarily evil; light is not always sublime. It is hard to say with certainty what gray represents. It can be vague or muddy. It is a kind of middle, in any case. "When we are happy, there is always a little sadness; and when we are sad we are also happy," says Butoh critic Nario Goda. This is acknowledged in the ambiguity of Butoh. As in all Butoh, the Sankai Juku enters the darkness and swallows it. It emerges with sublime stylization, a *shibui* clarification of elements, like the golden transparent liquid that results from the clarification of butter after it is boiled.

Shibui and the Sublime

Like the ballet, and like Bausch's dance theater, the Sankai Juku explores the sublime, but in a nondualistic modality that enfolds and unfurls its elements cyclically. If the sublime is the result, it is with a particular stylistic emphasis captured in the Japanese word *shibui*, an aesthetic concept that indicates quiet distinction, or restraint. The refined *shibui* also has inevitability about it, a subtle naturalness, even in its polish. It can call attention like the sour but natural taste of a lemon. Thus *shibui* can arrest the senses, but it does so without shouting. Japanese film critic and essayist Donald Richie defines *shibui* as a pleasant astringency and "severe good taste."[14]

When *shibui*'s proportions are magnified, small or subdued elements may become colorful, more visible, or perhaps even powerful. Such is the sublime as it opens upon the small, unusual, or overlooked detail like the glimpse of a spontaneously beautiful smile or distinctive face. A sublime *shibui* would be temperate, or it would not be *shibui*. It could also be pungent or magnetic, leading the senses. A sublime *shibui* would also overwhelm, or it would not be sublime. It would come without appositional strife and appear unexpectedly, like the spreading of a tree's shadow in moonlight or a figure of dust in the wind.

Although the sublime in Sankai Juku's aesthetic is not dualistically achieved as is the Kantian sublime, it is just as astounding. And as in Zen, it is ultimately unattached. Kantian disinterestedness might seem applicable here, since like Buddhism it also erases desire. Kant's term would not describe Buddhist detachment, however, especially that of Sankai Juku. The dance of Sankai Juku floats. Its detachment derives from the evanescent flow of nature and the transience of all things. It brings a flowing and sometimes bitter attention to the emergent and fading aspects of lived time. It augments the traces of historical time and our evolutionary body—of nature and culture entwining.

Jomon Sho, September 26, 1987

Amagatsu's concert-length work, *Jomon Sho: Homage to Prehistory* (Ceremony for Rainbow and Two Grand Circles, 1982) was performed at the Festival of New Dance in Montreal in 1986. As an East/West hybrid, it is like all Butoh, but it was one of the first dances to give Butoh an international visibility and status. *Jomon Sho* is curiously rooted in the ancient arts of Kabuki and Noh while making drastic departures from them. It is unmistakably Japanese in theatrical style, sparing nothing in effects—like the Kabuki. At the same time it is reserved—like Noh. Its *shibui* derives from a sinuous weave of brilliant theatrical elements with primal movement.

In the first of seven scenes, light dawns out of shadow; forms materialize gradually out of a dark void, as dancers' enfolded bodies compel the carefully drawn image. Amagatsu calls this place "hall of lasting breath" and "raining life." Four slate-gray figures appear first, huddled in the center of the floor and enclosed by two large cylindrical silver circles linked together as one. The figures show only their backs to the audience. Their shaven heads, which are tucked forward and hidden, emerge timorously, as the growing light reveals the shape of lean torsos.

The image is stark and bare. The white rice–powdered bodies are made universally one; individual ego is submerged in the whole. Cleanly suspended in the space just over the dancer's heads is a polished white egg-shaped object, a magic stone. Just as the back of their heads emerge to complete the line of the torso, the sitting figures with legs tightly folded topple over without anticipation. They hit the floor with a sudden thud, like the first rumble of a storm, or the fall of a giant footstep. As they roll over on their backs, their legs are free to tread midair. A growth of energy through the arms eventually lifts the figures, until they sit with arms and legs exploring upward. The lift continues toward the stone floating overhead.

The image peaks as the dancers are reaching (or pulled) upward.

Jomon Sho: Homage to Prehistory (1982), a dance conceived as
a ceremony for rainbow and two grand circles by Ushio
Amagatsu for his Butoh company Sankai Juku. *Photograph by
Setsuko Kato.*

Presently, the dancers are almost standing in the silver encir-clement. Splashes of light that have grown from the gray begin-ning give way to bright diffused light. Bodies materialize from gray outlines. Their mottled form turns glowing white as the center, both physical and spiritual, is reached. This point of ful-fillment is a preconscious surrender of fullness and freedom in mo-tion. It is almost pure form that we see, since personal features are diminished. The dancers progress from hidden inwardness to an exploration of upward and surrounding space as a single fea-tureless organism.

Other images throughout the work are closely wedded to the sparse, geometrically sculpted set, that creates an architectural environment or dwelling for the dance. Amagatsu's first solo ex-tends the development of the emergent beginning. This is inspired by sounds of the forest—or, as he calls it, our "forest-nature" pre-served, a dance of breath and muscle memory. Shortly after he en-ters the enchanted circle, four metal rods rain down in unison from above, spearing the four corners of the floor, piercing the be-ginning of his dance with a certainty and power mindful of the single-pointed simplicity of Zen.

One of the most visually stunning elements of the work com-mences with a tilting of the two circles around his solo.

They are lifted simultaneously and very slowly, each at one point, so as they are lifted, their angular connection to the ground increases. Amagatsu is enclosed in loops created by the double circles as they overlap and rise into vertical space. Geometry and nature meld as Amagatsu's arms fill the ascending and slowly revolving metal curves with the same curvature of arms. The shaping of human form and the shaping of objective material mirror and complement each other as the dance ripples like the surface of water circling the drop of a pebble. This is a solo of recognition. It is conscious of itself and aware of its surrounding, involved in deliberate play—weaving space, shape, and unity consciousness.

As Butoh reflects primordial emergence and spiritual awakening, it also accepts "the burden and bewilderment" of the body, as Kazuo Ohno has said. *Jomon Sho* acknowledges such understanding in a crawling dirge with mummylike creatures encased in bags and sprouting spines. As they inch their way across the stage, their mouths part and close to no avail, and they exit with the same labored undulations that have carried them slowly, eternally across the space. The slimy and stealthy are imagistically embodied and surrendered. (The movement also suggests fish.)

The dance evokes first utterance, the awe and wonder waiting behind words, as it commences anew from behind glass panes marking the four cardinal corners just outside the central circles. Once more a dawning light, as the dancers pluck up the sharp rods that have fallen and use them to probe the circular space. A dance of circles and sounding sticks materializes delicately.

Ohno likes to say that he does not agree with those who dance without emotion, voicing the same aesthetic perspective that initiated modern dance through Isadora Duncan and Mary Wigman. Like early expressionist dance, Butoh has sought to discover the spontaneous, emotional, responsive body. Likewise it has often turned to nature and organicism, ignoring highly evolved dance techniques and seeking first responses, feeling its way toward form. In *Jomon Sho,* culturally inherited dance manners are removed. The innately sensuous body is celebrated, but its presentational form is seldom raw. The rustic process aesthetic appreciated in Japan as *wabi sabi,* plain and austere beauty, appears—but briefly—only to transform into a sharp and glowing *shibui.*

This is realized finally in Amagatsu's solo performed in a long red skirt wrapping the hips, accenting his slate-white torso. A fullness of emotion infuses the dance, quixotic and consummate, yet never personalized. As throughout, the dance is disciplined and detailed, distinctively shaped in space and carved into time. Its rhythm is woven within sight of the enchanted stone and two mirrors remaining from the beginning. "In the beginning was the body," says Amagatsu. Fetal gestures, soft, pure, and minimal, juxtaposed with a feline jumping dance from all fours, landing on hands as well as feet, move the work to its conclusion. A shivering completes the dynamic mounting of energies. It cools with clear sounds of forest and birds as the other dancers enter. In the wake of their dance, a chorus of arms waves in boneless slow motion as though sublimely moved by water . . . incessantly . . . weaving . . . coaxing time. . . . "Time! Stand still!"[15]

My Mother's Face

Original Face
(Be a master
wherever
you are)

What was my face before my parents were born?

Zen koan (riddle)

July 16, 1988

When I danced in Natsu Nakajima's Butoh class in Toronto, I was keenly aware, at a critical moment toward the end of an hour and a half of impro-visational exercises, of a bodily emer-gence that I associated with birth. I experienced a purification and regres-sion of my limited self, a melting sen-sation of being unlimited. This was brought about by Nakajima's suggestion of "killing the body," softening the proud bearing and broad chest cultivated in extroverted Western dance. The class began with a slow meditative forward pace and softening of the breath to empty the torso. We carefully placed one foot in front of the other with eyes lowered and gradually opened an imagined third eye in the forehead.

From this beginning, which Nakajima called "being nothing" (nonbeing and emptiness), commenced a gradual appearance or filling of the body with breath as the dance moved smoothly forward. This was not an expansion of energy and persona, but more a dawning of being like the gathering of moonlight on water. A gentle cessation ended the continuum, what had become a floating walk. Without effort, eyes lifted to open easily and fully. There were several people observing the class. At the moment of being fully present, I experienced the bodily sensations and perhaps the primary meaning of emergence. I could not escape the on-looking gaze of the woman directly in front of me, a friend about the age of my deceased mother, though not at all of her particular disposition. My vision exploded softly, unexpectedly, to meet hers and the alert intuitive attention of the others watching. I felt unified with them and with the subtle ebb and flow of the other dancers, as a common dance of filling the body passed through us. All became a part of the moment and the hot tears of relief at the apex. Then a slow backward reversal of the process began, moving step by backward step into the third eye and the warm disappearance of nonbeing.

Killing the body (ego) and my chest's shell of pride, desiring nothing, letting go my self, I saw my mother's face.

Now that her death has given me her true face, I see my mother often. I am sublimely aware of her face in my own. I see her in the mirror, but even more in the light reflected. The individual features have vanished. Sometimes she comes to me through the faces of strangers, or through the faces of my friends in particular circumstances, especially at points of crisis, or when we are simply quiet together with no need for talk.

The luster of my daughter's face is in the reflection, and the remembrance of my grandmother's face on her death bed in a little red house on a dusty corner of the main street in a small farming town in Utah, the kind of town now all but disappearing, held mostly in memory. In that town, my grandmother raised a large family on meager resources. Her children were born in the small red house. Some of them died at birth. She died in her fifties, and so did my mother. Next year I will be fifty, but my life will not be short and a burden. The lives of my mother and grandmother have been given to me as a gift upon which to build independent worth—the stuff of long and happy lives.

I remember the enormity of my grandmother's daily chores: cleaning, cooking, and gardening—feeding children, chickens, pigs, and cows. For most of her adult life, she was pregnant. Sometimes, when I feel the weight and complexity of my professional tasks as a university professor, I think of her. And I remember how, with helplessness and guilt, my mother and her three sisters often talked of the endless work borne by their mother.

Mothers have a way of making us feel guilty, whether we deserve it or not; first, because they give up an enormous piece of themselves in giving birth, and second, because they always have so much work to do. If it's not housework, it's office work, volunteer work, busy work, needlework, and sometimes work to make ends meet. In some measure (perhaps emotional), we are in debt to our mothers. This is a debt we can never repay; at least, that is the feeling. If we are lucky, we are given ourselves without debts, since we didn't ask to be born in the first place, as children like to tell their parents in sudden flashes of insight or fits of indignation. If we are lucky, we are given (or we claim) the original blessing of our birth. The indebtedness of birth is erased through the grace of our mother's giving. When this giving is true grace, it is not another matter for indebtedness. At some point, the separate existential self and complex social self evolve, but always in creative tension with the ground for intimacy, the capacity for being-one-with that originated with the mother.

When we transcend our particular existential experience of "mother," the larger feminine principle, also called the Goddess, can begin to teach us. From Tara in Tibet to Isis in Egypt, she has many names. The metaphysics of the Goddess may not even be experienced in terms of one's own mother but is symbolic of qualities associated with the mythic feminine wherever it manifests in women and in men. In principle, our higher experience of mother is not existential—fraught with fearful possessiveness, worry, and guilt—but metaphysical; that is, full of grace. In one sense, the mother (the feminine) is open and allowing. She is yin (in Chinese philosophy), the receptive. She is a transparency and a mirror. She gives us to ourselves because she can be open, even as her body is physically open and receptive.

But, like the dark goddess Kali (in India) and Oya (in Nigeria), the Goddess is also a destroyer. She dances with fire. Like natural disasters, she uproots trees and tears them apart; she is a great leveler; she prepares the ground with her dance; she uproots the old and makes way for the new. In India, she is the "burning ground" of the heart, allowing the release of ego, preparing new ground for growth and insight. In Japan, she is the clearing away of ego that represents Zen emptiness. We pass through her to come back to ourselves, renewed, having gathered her metaphysical essence, the peace of our own arising and rebirth, just as ancient Demeter and her daughter Persephone passed through the dangers of the underworld and returned to bring forth the fruits of earth in springtime in Western mythology.

The mythical feminine, by her turbulent open/transformative character, allows the grace of separation (the arising of the unique self) and return (unification with other selves). We can observe this in nature's rhythms of growth, separation, and unification. Sometimes we can get out of our own way enough to see this happening (phenomenologically) in our own lives.

The interwoven yin/yang (archetypal) view of gender sees the masculine in both men and women as the urge toward individuation, separateness, the existential courage and loneliness of the singular man or woman, or the clarity of individual achievement. The dark feminine archetype is the ground of all achievement, however. All value emerges (gestates and is born) through her creative wisdom. Archetypal psychology makes male/female distinctions but sees them as necessary complements interacting within each person. It holds that masculine and feminine urges exist side by side in men and women, exerting polarized, creative tensions. They are interpenetrating aspects of being as they are represented in the psychology of Jung and in the *I Ching*, the Chinese book of changes and wisdom. Kazuo Ohno, whose classes and dances inform much of Butoh, including Nakajima's work, emphasizes a yin/yang perspective akin to that of Jung, teaching that each person contains the mother and the father, being born of both.

The feminine represents the urge toward bondedness and identification with others—in a word, love. *What we all want* is to love and be loved. Why then do we fail? The feminine in both men and women encompasses the complexities of intimacy. Do we not succeed in this some of the time? Through the mother, we learn about giving, sacrifice of ego, regeneration and renewal, even as these are contained in the feminine capacity of giving birth.

The face of my mother that appears to me now is beyond its finite features. And in it, I see the woman in every woman, the mother in men and women, the self in every self. What once engendered a desire for separation now appears as a mirror reminder of my inseparability from others. Others are in me, just as my daughter was, and I am in them. Nakajima's Butoh workshop in Toronto stirred this experience of oneness in me through a dance motif that deconstructed the armored shell of the body. Later, when I danced "Ohno's waters of life" in his class in Japan, it evoked once more the experience of the mother that Nakajima's workshop first introduced me to in her manner of "killing the body-ego."

The earthy soft aesthetic of Butoh makes conscious use of the mythopoetic mother principle. Most basically, the mother connects us to the great chain of life, to our sacred earth, and ultimately to our earthly body, to its pleasures, its powers, and its weaknesses. She is imperfect; therefore, she teaches love, tolerance, and forgiveness. She teaches us not merely to accept life and our body, but to *choose* them, to live (and to dance) in good faith in the light of who we are, not in imitation of an ideal body (an other). For to choose who we are, to welcome the body we are, is the beginning of health.

As deity, the Mother Goddess is not immutable and fixed. She has many faces and ages. As independent, she is virgin; as creative and generous, she is mother; as wise and unflappable, she is crone. As Yin in Asia, she is yielding, but still she is also symbolized in the I *Ching* as the teeth with courage to bite through difficult problems. As mysterious, she can be what she is not, melding oppositions, bringing understandings borne on intuition. In the past, her cultures have not been a matriarchal reverse of patriarchy, but cultures that emphasize partnership rather than dominance as a model (most recently the Minoan of Crete). She is Innana, Queen of Heaven, in Sumerian myth. Her other side is the rage of Ereshkigal, Queen of the Underworld. She is an aristocrat, and she is a toothless bag lady. In the gnostic gospels, she manifests in opposites, both whore and holy one, and like the answer to a Zen koan riddle, she is called Thunder, Perfect Mind. She has a dancer's name in the gospel of Valentinus: she is called Grace, the eternal silence.

As mythic, the Mother Goddess is all-containing nature, both nurturing and terrifying. This is why her face is in all faces. We all have a mother, and we all have a father; but the original bond, self-evident and accepting, peaceful and whole, is with and within the mother. She gives us, men and women alike, to our inner dance, the inside of things, our intuitive grasp of the world. She is our velvet-dark forgetting, unconditional love and forgiveness. Like the elusive *wabi-sabi* aesthetic in Japan, she is always transforming, thus never quite complete or arrested in time. One form dissolves into another. In her there is no death as such, only death and birth: regeneration. Her constellation of qualities has come to me time and again in the shadowy softness of Shinto shrines in the forest, the meditative Zen essence of Butoh, and its virgin/mother/crone transformations.

Butoh is dark, like all expressionism, but more than most it is consciously based in yin, also dark, the nondualistic Asian feminine principle that can change its character to incorporate or shift into its light-inspiring opposite. Butoh is an attempt to reclaim earthy, dark, and often bucolic values as they are quickly receding in industrialized postwar Japan and threatened around the world in the destruction of nature. In this it has much in common with ecofeminist concerns that embrace nature.[1]

Certainly there is also a sophisticated cultural overlay in Butoh, as it has been a theater of rebellion in vaunting cultural taboos, which has made it a troubling form of art to many. Like feminism, rebellious Butoh beginning with Hijikata's *Rebellion of the Body* is a cultural critique. Butoh would stand more solidly with ecofeminist values than with poststructural feminism that seeks to deny the mythical association of woman with nature and thus inadvertently sabotages our human responsibility to nature and the understanding of ourselves as part of nature. The founders of Butoh, Kazuo Ohno and Tatsumi Hijikata, danced in both male and female costume, not as female impersonators, but to release their feminine side and to call forth their mothers and sisters. When I feel divisions of gender blur and the otherness of others disappear in Butoh, my skin dissolves, and the universe wells up. This is a feeling I have come to appreciate as a manifestation of the mythic universal Goddess, the feminine deity symbolic of birth and the innocent unification of ourselves with nature. Like Butoh, she is often androgyne, yielding and transformational in her gender bending and existential tolerance for a wide range of expression. She is the bestowing mother, devoted to sustaining the earth and all of its creatures. She represents the free dance of our emotions and sensations. She is the gentle voice and tumultuous rage of nature in all of us. She longs for expression in daily life, in work and play, and especially in dancing. She is spontaneous.

As the scholarship on the Goddess continues to grow, it is most significant that she is becoming a symbol for reclaiming the darkness, as it originally represented fertility and transformation (not evil),[2] affirming the body and the earth (alive in our body) as sacred ground. The universal Goddess is not a symbol for matriarchy, for this is just the other side of patriarchy, and an exaggeration of either side represents destructive dominance. On an individual level, the Goddess stands for the inner dance of feminine and masculine principles in each person, and on a cultural level she stands for partnership between men and women.[3]

Dancing—and the attempt to come to terms with its processes in words—has given me insight into this universal metaphysical principle. The darkness of Butoh, the reverence for nature in Shinto and Zen, and the rustic aesthetic of ancient Japan with its nature goddess, Omikami Amaterasu, have given me concrete imagery for her.[4] The startling awakenings of Zen as they lie among matters of everyday occurrence express the mother's face: As *Suchness*, she is everywhere.

August 16, 1988

Early in the morning her smile returned to me during meditation, suffusing my being with a profound experience of solidity and invulnerability. Every doubt dispersed into the atmosphere to be replaced by what I can only describe as purity of being. I became as a rock, immovable in the surety of my existence, grounded and vibrating with *I am*. I sat more securely than I ever have with the universe, the universe in me. I saw my mother's face, not her features but her meaning, as before me passed the actual faces of women I know in their kindness, wisdom, and pain. It was then that I understood my larger self, the self beyond existential finitude, the self in all selves. It was still and peaceful in the darkness. In the vibrations of my tongue, I knew the power of silence.

And the darkness shall be the light,
and the stillness the dancing.

T. S. Eliot

Shards

Flower of Stone
(Thousands of
flowers carved
in rock)

I have some struggle in my heart. I like difficulty. If it were only easy, I could not do it. I think about oppositions: short and long, quick and slow, bright and dark. These elements are fighting, or next to each other, or shake hands, or love each other.[1]

Saburo Teshigawara

October 7, 1989

As Saburo Teshigawara studied mime and ballet, he became fascinated with the lines the body could make but was not satisfied with dance until he took a class with Butoh artist Kazuo Ohno, who encouraged him, as he has so many others, "to find his own dance."[2] Eventually, dance would become more for him than body lines in space. In his explorations, he initiated an original dance aesthetic, not simply a phase of Butoh. It is close to historic modern in its formal shaping of choreography and also relates to the American postmodern in its deconstructive erasure of overt emotion. Teshigawara's dance is, however, still expressionist and symbolic, as has been a defining thrust of Butoh. He has developed a cool objective style that distinguishes him from Butoh, but its influence is nevertheless evident. Like Ohno, Teshigawara proceeds from a dream body. He is not mundane (in the everyday sense of Min Tanaka, for instance).

Transparent and emptied—from his whitened hair to his face and clothes—Teshigawara enters the cloudy field of his dance theater work *Ishi-No-Hana* (*Flower of Stone*). A bleached postmodern plainness is apparent in his white shirt, tailored cotton pants, and lace-up shoes. He might even be a jazz dancer, but the blood seems drained from his pale frame, and his aesthetic (while astonishing) is not extraverted. As in Butoh, he draws freely from both Western and Eastern symbolism and is emotionally distilled in gesture; although distorted Butoh facial expressions are not even suggested.

Critics have claimed that he is producing a blend of Butoh sensitivity and postmodern elements, a "postButoh" dance.[3] Indeed, his use of rocks on stage recalls Kei Takei's primal works that have also have been termed Butoh and postmodern, but Teshigawara's are more smoothly theatrical, less raw than Takei's, particularly when she invokes primate human origins. (In more recent works, such as *Here to Here* and NOIJECT in 1995, Teshigawara continues to distance himself from Butoh.)

Blue rocks arranged to create corridors on the floor and a pile of broken glass strewn with gold sculpt the space of *Ishi-No-Hana*. Teshigawara moves haltingly into the eerie beauty, like a sleepwalker. His movements are uncanny and unfamiliar. Sometimes they flow; sometimes they jerk. The shoulders are held in tight solid blocks as the legs wobble, then melt as the legs stiffen. His style is consistently inconsistent—controlled, but let go. He moves gracefully beyond volition like a paper doll being crumpled up, and then, for no reason, pressed out at odd times. Sometimes the figure folds and trembles all over, or just in certain joints, more moved than moving.

The piece is built of episodes, delving into energies and images. Four men who provide a musical ground bass repetition or quartet drone for the work intrude suddenly upon Teshigawara's solo. Sayoko Yamaguchi, an elegant woman in a red kimono, carries a stuffed fish wrapped in gold. She enters with it, pacing demurely. Costumed in contrast to her, the men are in Western dress like Teshigawara: white shirts, black pants and ties, with blocky black lines on their shirt backs like a stack of yang lines along the spine.

The men crouch, coiled and ready to move among the rocks. They move fast with intermittent bursts of power, thrusting toward the sky, then falling down on their sides. Oblivious to them, the woman carries the fish ceremoniously. Occasionally, she also falls down on her side, unexpectedly—then continues her journey with smoothly restrained careful steps. When she comes close to Teshigawara's supernatural figure, he helps her unwrap the gold strands from the fish.

This is a dream world inhabited by objects from daily life and nature that obtain transcendent qualities as attention is called to unusual uses of them in the dance. Two of the four men who weave in and out of the work enter on bicycles, invading a tender duet, blunting it midmotion as they fall, bicycles and all. In one frozen scene, there are several exaggerated objects reposing in silence. The dancers' movement is fought in fitful holes of stony stillness. Gradually the faint sound of insect buzzing wafts over the picture and accumulates to a roar, as the stage tableau evolves into a fully composed and statuesque collage. The woman now holds a fish grown much fatter than the original. The ashen figure waits, and the four men perch like a steely choir of warriors. There is also machinery, a large reel-to-reel tape deck upright in the middle. Off to the side, a small dancer, Kei Miyata, stands on a stool with an enormous dragonfly balanced on top of her head. The dragonfly tilts and sways slightly from its connection to her head, the only visible motion.

As the scene dissembles, she removes her dragonfly headdress and commences a charming song, a repetitious children's jingle, punctuated with pauses and falls. Falling down is indeed the signature movement of the work. Relentlessly, dancers collapse to the floor on one side, then quickly recover a centered stance, to fall and get up again and again. One section rivets particular attention

In *Ishi-No-Hana* (Flower of Stone), Saburo Teshigawara hunches up in an oblique, squeezed gesture while Sayoko Yamaguchi peers out at the audience through a bicycle wheel. *Photograph by Nobuyoshi Araki.*

on this existential motif. The four warriors become welded together, falling into the stone corridors, eventually devouring the stage space, throwing themselves fiercely into the floor over and over again, almost hitting their heads on the blue stones as they traverse the dangerous pathways.

Pushing limits still further, the dancers pound the rocks into the floor. Warriors paw and stamp together with the wild energy of horsemen in a pack. There are also tender moments, as in one duet when Teshigawara breaks the fall of the woman in red, catching her to hold a precarious pose. Sublime releases follow the extremes of falling and pounding. At one point, soft welcome singing breaks out like a shaft of sun through a thundercloud. A chorus of five dancers in red weave a broad mass of successional flow through space.

Teshigawara is alone in the pile of ground and broken glass in a remarkable episode near the end. There is no music, just the sound of his sifting through the glass, protected by his shoes and clothes. In contrast to the episodes that build and crash, this one chills. Here the dancer's background in mime is abstracted freely. He examines a small pane of glass, looks through it, then smashes and stomps it into the pile. He repeats this, and we know the glass is real, as we hear it shatter. He kneels and finally beds down in the glass, finding a few larger pieces, placing one in his mouth. As he extricates himself, a little blood appears on the knee of his white pants, and the queasy uneasiness of broken glass remains.

Other dancers enter the space; the men begin falling again. A female dancer drifts among them. In a final fall, the men stop just short of their heads falling to the floor. The fall is held there in-complete, with the head and one leg suspended barely off the ground. The dancers fight the air as they fall. Suddenly the woman kneels and reaches out to touch the top of a falling head. Dancers freeze in this position, as a female chrysalis wrapped in red silk unwinds slowly from the back corner across the stage, creating a sea of silk in her wake.

The pale figure from the glass pile trails her, gathering the silk in and finally rewrapping her. The interspaced sounds swell, then stop abruptly in the middle, arresting the dance. It seems unfinished, as though it might commence at the slightest provocation. The sharp and wounding dance recalls the black worrisome bird for which Teshigawara named his company, *Karas*, the raven.

I distill Teshigawara's *Ishi-No-Hana* further:

Gaunt, the dream wails;
insect buzzing bathes the dance.
Falling bicycles,
horsemen, thrash blue shards
and glass aglint with gold.

He flowers,
and trembles;
an empty wave jerks through him.

The dragonfly tilts
and says on her head of daily life and nature—
cut, a fat fish, a red sea.

For no reason,
God! press out the wrinkles
here and there;
sound sifting and shuffling
through the glass.

Empty
Land

Empty Land
(All is nothing)

October 26, 1989

Natsu Nakajima's work accomplishes a completeness of dramatic expression and formal design. Her theatricality universalizes. Intermingling darkness and light, her dances are besouled, demonic, transformative, and magical. Nakajima has universalized the human face with white rice powder as Wigman did through masks. Individual features melt, the personal is derealized; Nakajima's white face is no one and everyone. Just as good masks change expressively according to the wearer and angle of presentation, Nakajima finds many others and angles within herself as mask.

Her visionary work, *Sleep and Reincarnation From Empty Land*, was performed at La Mama theater in New York City. It is about New York and Japan, but not specifically. It exists in dream time somewhere. It contains the cool smooth continuity of Japanese Noh theater, Noh's profoundly concentrated attention to the smallest details of motion, and a flair for color, line, and adornment akin to Kabuki theater. It is equally Western, as lyrical and passionate as opera. The music is both Western and Asian, including German lieder, synthesizer, violin, piano, organ, Japanese harp, Indian tabla drum, and such natural sounds as whale cries. Her theatricality is transcultural. It blends contrasts to move beyond them. Nakajima's work is an extended meditation on life, death, and transfiguration. She dances the many faces of woman—as a tooth-mother bag lady and a goddess of love. Her partner Yukio Waguri is a shaman: part animal, part human, erotic, strong, and tender. With the supporting international ensemble of dancers that Nakajima trained in New York, she and Waguri weave a mosaic of divine love that evokes Japan's ancient quietude—not its modern speed but its reverence for nature through Zen and Shinto. As in her earlier work *Niwa*, Nakajima draws upon the goddess of Japan from ancient to modern times, Omikami Amaterasu. Ancient Japan and modern America meld in *Sleep and Reincarnation*, a dance of hope, arising paradoxically from the degrading filth of New York City streets.

In the first section, "Mosquito Curtain and Shallow Dream," Nakajima trails a soft stream of transparent material wrapped around her shoulders, a white robe with a long train that unfurls the entire length of her gliding entrance from the darkened far corner to a central lighted pool. She emerges like a prayer, her face radiant, gradually turning upward as if to absorb some heavenly blessing. Blue tinges the end of her long drape, fading upward into pale delicate shoulders and her rice-white face. Carefully she traces a circle on the fringes of the light, pacing smoothly into the center, creating a billowy cloud of cloth into which she descends. She moves gently down into the vortex of the pool with the fragility and clarity of a perfected Japanese doll, every detail of facial expression a new instance of emotion, as though something of human history welled up and moved through the face. Sorrow and envy, pleasure and loss mingle. Playing between light and shadow, her face melts now and then from the warmth of expressiveness to coldly carved gestures. Her slightest shivers are well delineated, seen and felt at a distance. They float in space. As she comes to rest, her body is given up to sleep, and the mythical dream time of the dance begins; slow, eternally patient time.

"*Jiraiya*," the phantom creature of thunder who can vanish at will, is danced by Waguri. He wears a golden loin cloth and a sculpted gold headdress to frame his chalk face. Red knee bands encircle his bare legs. Waguri dances *Jiraiya* with demonic and animal powers, a witness to nature, infused with it, helpless against it, one with it. His fingers curl, he jumps high in the air with legs curled under. His whole body convulses. It twists and shudders, stomps and stalks. Pointing an accusatory finger then fastening it to his forehead like a horn, Waguri jabs and falls. His body is pummeled by the thunder, by bullets and bombs. The intense sounds of drumming propel his spasms and thrusts. More hurled upward than leaping into space, he seems thrown by outside forces, and a shout rips from his throat as he vanishes into the blackout.

In "Distant Landscape," the next long section of the work, poetic images are developed. Dances come and go like a stream moving through changing terrain, growing wide at certain points with the ensemble dancing, then narrowing into specific solos. The landscape is sparse, and each dance is like a Japanese minimalist painting, accomplished with only a few strokes. The dances are not abstract in impression, however; they clearly project character, both human and animal, and contain concrete images from nature. The ensemble first appears wrapped in tentlike triangular costumes that unroll from around their bodies as they walk softly backward toward the audience. The entire movement consists of this simple backward approach toward the stage front with only the backs of feet and ankles visible from under the costumes. A slight rise and fall in the stepping is dotted with full stops. Further oppositional play of shrouded figures, shrinking and stretching, balances the stage space. The costumes unroll like scrolls as the dancers approach, appearing larger and more finely detailed as they get closer. Finally we see formal scenes painted across the top and bottom of the costumes like miniature landscapes unfurling on parchments.

"Stone Play" calls to mind the quiet of a Japanese stone garden. Nakajima's costume for this solo echoes the tent or treelike costumes of the departing ensemble. She wears a cone of paper around her head and a simple paper garment. There is a ghostly transparency in her entrance. She makes her way to a raised platform where several small rocks are arranged, more or less in a circle. She settles into the rocks and begins to pick them up, holding each one, examining them quietly with full attention. One can feel the gentle weight and smoothness of rocks in her small hands. She stacks them three at a time. The unadorned plainness of this contemplative play is captivating. Eventually she removes the square of paper framing her head and folds it. As she places each rock carefully on the folded paper, it becomes a plate. Gradually she removes the paper outer garment to move into the center light, and a new incarnation emerges dressed in long sleeves and a tiered skirt, not specific to any period or place. With her torso, arms, and head, Nakajima dances life's ambivalences, alternating between hope and despair. Most poignantly her arms reach, then droop and dangle in futility.

In the next image, called "Walk of the Dead," the ensemble moves evenly across the back of the stage, spinning out a long line of motion like a single brush stroke. The dancers are anonymous in neutral tunics and turbans, and their faces are dusty, indistinguishable. There is also a dusty beauty in their movement as they carry themselves without accent or pause across the width of the space with feet pressing slowly forward in continuous contact with the floor. Rotations of the feet, toes together then heels to-

Natsu Nakajma's "Stone Play" from *Empty Land*, choreographed in New York City in 1989. *Photograph by Nourit Masson-Sekine.*

gether, move them in a seamless direction to the side. The upper body states curves in gestural contrast to the minimal foot motion. The dancers move in the distance like an apparition, dissolving from one side of the space to the other. Their journey is undifferentiated. The movement is repetitive, monotone, and elegant.

Waguri's dance, "Birds and Animals," moves somewhere between plant and animal life. Most of all it reflects the animal source of words, their rootedness in the body. Waguri's movements are often gnarled, especially his hands, as the wrists arch upward and the fingers curl into claws. He seems all wrists and knuckles. This animal would speak if it could. Its throat stretches, but no sounds come. Waguri descends to the floor on all fours and his hands melt into hoofs. Tenuously he paws and stirs the earth, like an absentminded creature intuitively searching the ground, then moving on to whatever catches its attention next. Movement is focused on details and nuance of change, as it represents the expressiveness of animals, the wordless vivid world of nature. Waguri's beast weeps, roars, flies, perches, and hovers; sometimes it jerks upward into the air as though being pulled by a puppeteer. He is wrapped in a long red skirt with some fur around his neck, and a bird's nest crowns his head. Trance and possession enter the dance, effecting a metamorphosis, and Waguri's costume in its mixture of primitive textures with smooth sophistication lends substance to the transformation.

"Arrow Woman" contrasts distinctively with Nakajima's other solos. Here she shows sharp and penetrating qualities, the tough yang attributes of character—whereas the softer yin sensibilities dominate in her dances overall. The total impression of *Sleep and Reincarnation*, like *Niwa* (*The Garden*), is more yin in its yielding grace. It accepts the cycles of life and death. "Arrow Woman" is tight and minimal, danced to syncopated orchestral jazz. Nakajima's costume and demeanor suggest Martha Graham, as do the central contractions of her motions. The dance is insistent and percussive, with tense torso movement throughout. Nakajima presses an arrow lengthwise between her two palms for most of the dance with fingers outstretched from the tip to the top of the arrow, pressing the tip into one hand from the force of the other. The symbolism of pain is obvious here. Her body is carried toward the pain at moments, and sometimes pushed away.

She moves forward on the diagonal line she established in the beginning (as in *Niwa*). We see this as a life line, a journey traveled again and again, but with ever new obstacles and yearnings. The dance bursts into larger jabs, torso thrusts, and head tossing. It becomes more abandoned as it develops, but never loses its hard-edged contractive essence. As it reaches the center of the space and moves toward an end, the legs become more prominent, stepping wider. One leg is thrown out from under the skirt, occasionally stabbing the floor. Finally the arrow falls from one hand to the other. Nakajima takes the arrow and whirls it. Her white face passes through ecstasy, pain, and laughter.

Floating figures in "Dream of Whales" are as neutral (and universal) as they were in "Walk of the Dead." The dancers recline on their sides with their heads wrapped, wearing simple tunics draped over long pants. They are still for a long time, adrift in the silence, except for an occasional animal sound in the distance, a muffled growl or cry. In unison the dancers lift one arm gently overhead, then curve it down to touch the top of the head with two fingers, deliberately lifting and reversing the arm slowly to return the hand to rest. This gesture is repeated, a single unison stroke in space, overlapped once or twice with plaintive whale calls. All at once the dancers lift one leg, floating it upward, outstretched but with the foot truncated, the ankle leading the motion, reminiscent of a tail. Some evolutionary memory is exposed in the audience's empathetic response. The scene evokes our kinship with whales, their immensity and serenity, *their sublimity*, their mystery and majesty.

The final dance in "Distant Landscape," the first half of the concert, is Nakajima's solo, "Plum Blossom Dance." She enters on her well-traveled diagonal path. This time she wears a long, dark, and simple straight dress of rough material and carries two stems of plum blossoms. German lieder plays in the background. There is an air of loneliness about her. She might be any age, but images of old age are most evident. She crouches in the center, lays down her branches on the floor in front of her, and begins to warm her hands over them as though they were a fire. Her eyes blink, and her facial expressions conjure up images that seem to come as remembrances out of the past.

Nakajima has dedicated "Distant Landscape" to her teacher Tatsumi Hijikata. Her program notes include a letter he wrote to her when she embarked on her first world tour. One phrase, in particular, speaks of Nakajima's plum blossom solo:

Natsu Nakajima's "Distant Landscape" from *Empty Land*. *Photograph by Nourit Masson-Sekine.*

Go with the Japanese woman's old withered breasts, go as a suffering pilgrim from the low class, and crouching. Go with your love which you tear and throw. . . . I only stick out my tongue under the rain.

The last half of the concert, composed of eight parts that create one extended dance, is called "Newspapers" and is dedicated to New York City. The dances are not conceived as separate entities as in the first half. They are interdependent in structure and meaning, and the costumes remain almost constant throughout. Great swirling tents of newspapers taped together encircle the neck to cover the whole body. They extend outward and down to the floor, leaving just the head visible. The anonymous uniformity of the costumes with their rustling sounds permits a myriad of imagery to arise. The newspapers are surprisingly suggestive. One creature scuttles about like a robot on automatic; comic elements develop. Often the ensemble of newspapers is blown and piled up by the wind, like stray newspapers on pavement.

When all the dancers rush and move about together in semi-darkness, the papers sound like the ebb and flow of the sea. They become as intertwined as seaweed, as gauzy and sticky. Mountains form in a storm of paper, then become still for a while. Suddenly, dancers stoop down in unison, quickly gathering the newspapers around them for shelter with faces all eyes peeking out. At times the figures seem to be rummaging through garbage, then they huddle together seeking warmth against the cold. One cannot escape the obvious allusions to New York City streets as heaps of

Natsu Nakajima's "Newspapers" from *Empty Land*. *Photograph by Nourit Masson-Sekine*.

human refuse pile up. The music swells often into a kind of howl-ing. Nakajima has a solo that evokes madness. Her body is rigid beneath the newspapers, drumming tiny bouncing steps in one place with the heel jamming into the floor sharply. Finally Naka-jima returns to the platform where she had previously played with stones, now exhausted, used up by the dance. Slowly she emerges from under the newspaper cape, like a butterfly from a cocoon. She is dressed in a celestial white simple tunic draped over pants and a contrasting turban of soft lavender.

Waguri enters from a back corner and echoes her emergent movements in the background. His costume is like hers. As he moves closer and enters the central light, his movements become a perfect complement of Nakajima's bodily held shapes, full of reverence with gentle hand gestures and leanings in the torso. They move away from each other holding the center, like the opening of a lotus blossom. The last shape is of outspreading white wings, as Nakajima and Waguri kneel together, arms outstretched in a downward curve. Their heads bow to touch the ground as the lights fade.

Their final bow is choreographed. In Japanese style, Nakajima and Waguri kneel, arranging their gowns around them with one deft motion, then bow to the floor with hands framing their heads. The complement of their movements and their identical costumes create an androgyne ending. As the ensemble enters to take their bows, we see them out from under the refuse of newspaper also in white pants with overtunics. Quickly they lay large ripe pumpkins on the stage. Then like angels they encircle Nakajima and Waguri. The final symbolism bridges earth and spirit, autumn's ripeness and white light.

Before the first blink of time
birds and animals think
weep, roar, fly

American Mother and Shinto

Dragon
(Dragon)

May 6, 1990

My Japanese friend and I took the train to Mito City where she had re-served rooms for us at Keisei Hotel. That evening we had *shabu shabu* at the hotel—my favorite Japanese food of thinly sliced beef and vegetables that is cooked in basting broth and served in a pot at the table. (I allow myself beef as a condiment on such rare *shabu shabu* occasions.) We talked intimately over cognac at the roof garden club afterward. I remember this as the kind of girl talk I know so well with American friends.

She told me about the inside and outside exclusionary character of Japanese life that creates an ever-narrowing central focus on the inside. Even families have those on the inside and those on the outside. She also talked of her first lover, and how she became ill when he married someone else. It took her years to understand that she was in love with a ghost, she told me, not a real person. It seemed I had heard this story before, and I was reminded of how much women—even successful professionals—are held in the thrall (and bondage) of love and romance.

The next day Humie, my adopted Japanese daughter (one of several), joined us, and we walked in and around the school for samurai, a famous landmark in Mito City. It was bare, cold, and simple with a few pictures of the major teachers. Just an occasional scroll on the wall, or a painting accomplished with lean strokes of muted earth colors: gray-brown and gray-pink. The smooth tatami mats joined with the gold ribbon pattern of the Tokogawa shogunate felt cool and purifying to my bare feet.

In the afternoon, we saw a student dance concert at the local college—amateurs dancing for the fun of it. For the most part, the program was squared-off disco style jazz tinged with commercial routines and Michael Jackson imitations. As parents flooded the stage at the end with bouquets for their daughters, an earthquake struck the city, rocking the very large building and shaking us badly.

Earthquakes are common here, but this was bigger than usual, interrupting train travel. So Humie and I waited for two hours in the cold as we stood in line for the train to Itako town where I was to visit her extended family. I put my arms around Humie who was shaking from the cold by now. I seemed more resilient for the time being, and I suspected she was also shaking from the apprehension of having me as a guest. So much preparation goes into hospitality in Japan—city or country.

Her brother-in-law Hiro met us at the train and drove us to her parent's modest store in Itako town. In the small living quarters behind the store with her brothers, uncle, and aunt, I was served the beloved green tea—O cha—and green tea cake, and admired the tall bamboo growing in a grove outside the window. Humie's mother presented me with a present made by an old man in Ohno village, a plaque covered with sea shells, the central scene being that of three turtles on top of each other in a pile—papa, mama, and baby turtle, or some kind of family arrangement. We never really got it sorted out linguistically.

Humie's family of six managed to live in very cramped quarters at the back of the store, a general store selling food and sundries. Her mother and father worked there every day, even weekends and holidays. Her mother also cooked and cared for the family; they did not apologize for their circumstances. Humie had gotten an education at Ibaraki University and was a school nurse with her own small room in Itako town. Her sister was married, and her two brothers were still at home.

After tea and the giving of presents, I was taken to the ladies' room outside. It was clean, and chilly. Then we left for the main event of the stay—a party in my honor at her grandfather's charming farmhouse in Ohno village, where as Humie assured me "the toilet is indoors."

I sat cross-legged on my pillow where I was seated across from Humie's father. Humie sat on my left. The low table was a beautiful polished deep brown-red color, and an additional table had been added to accommodate the large gathering. Humie's entire family of uncles, aunts, and cousins came to meet me, each one bowing and making special greetings. I bowed back of course. All of this took place from a kneeling position around the table during a large meal of special condiments and exquisitely arranged platters of sushi. Humie's father and I poured each other's beer (I was told this should be the protocol), and the others followed.

Toward the end of dinner, Humie announced to me, "your whiskey is ready if you want it." Seems the Japanese associate Americans with whiskey. I told them I would prefer sake (rice wine). I noticed her uncle was having plenty, and he was happy to oblige me. This uncle had also set up an amplifier and mike for karaoke—the Japanese pastime of singing into a mike along with recordings of popular songs, in this case Japanese and American, the lyrics being provided in a songbook. This gives the more gregarious the opportunity to perform with orchestral backup and a mike, and it makes for great fun at parties. I had already experienced karaoke at Japanese restaurants in America, most notably in Las Vegas where they take tacky seriously. My daughter was persuaded to sing by the locals, and I danced with a local "ballroom expert."

Karaoke in a Japanese village was something I could never have imagined—country, the ancestors, and technology—quaint manners and pop, with the grandparents and young generation participating together. They wanted me to sing a solo: a Frank Sinatra song, "My Way." Well, I wanted to sing "My Way," but the songbook was in Japanese, and I don't know the words by heart. "Could we hear just your voice then," they said "with no accompaniment." They turned off the machines, and sat in silence while I searched my memory for any Sinatra song I might know. I remembered well a song from my father's repertory of love songs—I knew an oldie. Maybe Sinatra sang it, or Bing Crosby (it was Alice Fay, I found out later).

I started to sing, a little quiet at first (but I had the mike), "You'll never know just how much I love you. . . ." The talkative uncle closed his eyes to hear better. I sang it through to the end, also closing my eyes sometimes, to let the words come by themselves. Well, it wasn't Sinatra, but there was much applause. The uncle picked up on "I love you" from the song and kept saying it to me periodically after that with a twinkle in his eye.

There were many questions about my husband then. "Wasn't he lonely without me?" And "did I think he was being faithful?" Humie was translating back and forth furiously. They insisted I should call him at their expense right then and there, but I convinced them that he would be teaching school (it was daytime at home), so we dropped it.

I coaxed the uncle to sing. Then Humie's mother sang. They sang into the mike with musical backup—some popular Japanese songs. Lastly Humie's brother-in-law who sings with a band sang the awaited-for Sinatra's "My Way," and in English. We shouted and applauded.

Humie could see the party was getting out of hand, and she whisked me off to a hot Japanese bath. After I had showered clean, the soaking bath was waiting in a deep wooden tub. The water was so hot we had to pour in a lot of cold to even put a finger in without scorching it. When I came back to the party room, it had become our bedroom. Humie and I had futons there. She gave me a long back rub, and told me I was her American mother.

In the morning, we woke to a two-hour long breakfast of sea vegetables in miso, fish, tofu, and many other small delicious dishes I couldn't identify. This was a typical country breakfast that tourists pay about $75 for on the Ginza in Tokyo. Grandmother served. I was surprised how she managed in spite of her greatly stooped posture and halting gait. The rice paper windows were slid open, a chilly breeze circulated the fresh green smell of the garden with its small waterfall. A warmer under the table kept us cozy in our cross-legged postures sitting on the polished wooden floor.

There is a very small ancient Shinto shrine in Ohno village named Tsubaki Shrine after the pink *tsubaki* flower. Humie and I walked there after breakfast. It was early, the sun was out and the weather mild. There were high hedges on the road and an occasional farmhouse in view. When we arrived, we paused under the simple wooden Shinto gate and entered along the silent path leading to the little shrine of dark brown surrounded by dense woods. I remembered that Shinto preceded Zen in Japan as the religion of the Goddess. We were alone with the birds and insects; the smells were fragrant and damp.

I have visited larger shrines, usually with crowds of people in Japan. Here at Tsubaki Shrine in Ohno Village with Humie, the nature essence of Shinto welled up inside me, and I thought how Shinto reverences nature in its wildness. "God is here," I said to Humie.

Because I love dragons, those awesome animals of damp caves and windy woods, Humie took my picture under the dragon carving—the only decoration on the shrine.

Liebe

Susanne
Linke
and
Toru
Iwashita

Love
(Love)

In a space of fifteen days in Tokyo, I saw three dances titled *Liebe* (*Love*). One, by German soloist Susanne Linke, is actually two dances in one. It includes a reconstruction of Dore Hoyer's *Liebe*, one of the last dances of the original expressionist period in Germany. Linke revives this dance, then adds her own neo-expressionist *Liebe* in response. The third version of *Liebe* is an unlikely "karaoke expressionism" by Toru Iwashita. He dances with Sankai Juku but is developing an aesthetic less polished and more mundane in his solos.

Linke's work is performed as a tribute to Hoyer. It is not Butoh but has close ties. Linke's new expressionism and that of Butoh both revive early developments in expressionist modern dance. *Liebe* and its Germanic source (as the word indicates) is the indirect subject of Iwashita's dance and Linke's, but *liebe*, love, is not directly expressed in these dances; instead, it is the foil for an immense struggle, the image that propels struggle toward catharsis.

The juxtaposition of these three works makes the expressionist basis of Butoh clear. Contrary to expectations evoked by the title, these dances are not pleasing, and definitely not comforting. They are built on shadowed moods where emotions mix; hope and anguish intermingle.

Susanne Linke in Tokyo

April 29, 1990

Susanne Linke and I were students together at the Wigman School in 1964–65 in Berlin; ours was a class of about twenty dancers. I still have a film of our dances for Wigman's seventy-ninth birthday that also includes other festivities.[1] Linke's dance is youthful, soft like a caress, with palms pressed together and the back of the hands brushing each cheek toward the end. When I saw her dance twenty-two years later in Montreal, I was not surprised that a fuller spectrum of experience appeared in her work. We talked over dinner then, and now again in Tokyo after her performance of her homage to Dore Hoyer.

"Who am I?" the existential question that Mary Wigman sought to answer through dance, is Linke's quest as well. Her dances seem a means toward self-disclosure. They are not merely personal or private explorations, however. Linke's dances speak to the human condition that concerned continental existentialism in Germany and France, the courage of solitude in the face of loneliness and alienation and the responsibility of confronting the bewilderment of our inescapable freedoms.

I believe that Linke's dances grapple with freedom and ethical problems of feminine immanence, the condition that philosopher Simone de Beauvoir explored in her question, "Why is woman the other?" Why is woman to be overshadowed and forever transcended by another ego (conscience) that is more essential and sovereign? Linke's agonistic poetics derive from a feminist conscience. They are inner dramas of conflict, struggles toward freedom, both moral and spiritual.

Linke seeks a fullness of spirit in her dances that she identifies with Asia. "I feel closer to Indians than to Westerners," she says. Like Kazuo Ohno, she deplores intellectually derived dance, especially that of Merce Cunningham. She admires the honesty of Chandralekha. In the expressive and revolutionary tradition of Isadora Duncan, Mary Wigman, Dore Hoyer, and Pina Bausch, Linke interrogates sexual and social stereotypes.

Feminine immanence is apparent in Linke's aesthetic, yet her dances are not literal or didactic. They seldom drive so clearly to clench a point. Linke's *Affecte* (1987) is a special case in point. It is a full-length concert containing the dance *Liebe*. It explores freedom and limitation lived within the self and between the self and others. *Affecte* is conceived as a duet with her partner Urs Dietrich. As homage to the inspirational Dore Hoyer, it recapitulates her themes. Hoyer's were dances of protest, dances of mystery, dances of death and contingency. Linke's concert, *Affecte*, is also a record of the final tragic chapter of the original expressionist dance. Hoyer, claimed by Wigman to be her only legitimate heir, took her own life on the eve of 1968. She left a letter to her longtime friend and artistic associate, Mathilde Thiele. She remembered how they had lived together like "vagabonds and squatters" through the Second World War and its aftermath. True to the existentially committed aesthetic of German expressionism, she had lived in her dances, and would die with them.

I saw Hoyer dance in Berlin in 1965, when I was a student with Linke at the Wigman School. Thiele was our principle teacher there, aside from Wigman herself. Thiele is eighty-four now and lives only fifty miles from me on Lake Ontario. I spend a great deal of time with her, listening to her remembrances of dance and war and sharing her memorabilia. Thiele danced with Gret Palucca, Mary Wigman, and Dore Hoyer, the three central personalities who shaped German expressionist dance amid the turmoil, disgrace, and disintegration of their homeland.

(As I update this essay in 1996, Thiele has just turned ninety, also the age of Kazuo Ohno. She has a snapshot of Ohno's teacher Takaya Eguchi, when he was studying with Wigman. Eguchi, as explored in the introduction, was influential in shaping new dance in Japan after his return from Germany. When Thiele and

I look over her photographs from this period, I can't help but see Harald Kreutzberg in the background of Butoh. The flowing robes and shaven heads of Sankai Juku resemble Kreutzberg. Sankai Juku also recalls the simple draping robes and polished heads of monks, but their dramatic flair is closer to Kreutzberg. I also associate Ohno with Kreutzberg's flowing abstract expressionism, so I was not surprised to find out that Ohno took up the study of dance with Eguchi after seeing Kreutzberg dance in 1934.[2])

Hoyer died at the end of the year 1967, at the dawning of 1968, an apocalyptic year with political assassination in America (Robert Kennedy and Martin Luther King), race riots (Miami and Los Angeles), student activism (the Kent State murders), and a Germany heavily laden with the West's nuclear arsenal and still divided. Modern dance was becoming postmodern in America, turning away from emotional motivation through the influence of Merce Cunningham and Yvonne Rainer. In Europe, Hoyer was the last ember of expressionism. Ballet (in both its classical and contemporary modes) defined the dance aesthetic in Europe, and modern dance had moved too far from expressionism to appreciate Hoyer.

My consciousness of the early expressionist dance—its spiritual search and self-searching, its beautiful ugliness, was revitalized by Linke's *Affecte*, and my memory of seeing Hoyer dance. I remembered mostly the emotional shades of her dancing, the piercing qualities and bleak contours hiding a vulnerable softness underneath. The most engrossing aspect of Linke's *Affecte* is her juxtaposition of the clearly etched emotions in Hoyer's *Affectos*

Humanos with a blurring of these very same emotions in her own work. Hoyer's original *Affectos Humanos* (1961) was based on five emotional dispositions: vanity, avidity, anxiety, hate, and love (*liebe*).

In the first half of her concert, *Affecte*, Linke dances her reconstruction of Hoyer's suite from a film of the work. In the last half, she dances her own choreography with Dietrich on the same themes. The exposed and vulnerable *Dolor*, Linke's dance on Hoyer's death, is a solo that connects the two halves. The critical values that ground Linke's work are structural as the parts relate aesthetically and historically. *Affecte* is a reverberation of Hoyer's *Affectos Humanos*. It rings with the same emotions. We see them in aesthetic-historical perspective with contemporary innovations filtered through Linke's persona and twenty years' passing.

The reconstructed Hoyer solos are bare and ascetic. In them, Linke expresses love (and pain) in precise movement. *Liebe* in Hoyer's original solo dance is a skillfully performed hand dance from a sitting position, while Linke's duet with Dietrich on *Liebe* is flung into space, telling a story of love intermingled with brutality and death. The hands in Hoyer's choreography are like shadow puppets of doves. As the hands turn, supple wrists move like necks, and the fingertips become beaks in conversation, moving together and apart, telling a story of love's awakenings and illusions, approaches and recriminations.

Linke dances Hoyer's *Liebe* as a remembrance of something held inside. She is dressed in pink with soft bare arms, but the skull cap she wears disallows such comfort. When she faces the audi-

Dora Hoyer in her expressionist work "Angst" from *Affectos Humanos*, a cycle of dances that she began in Germany in 1961. *Photograph by Siegfried Enkelman/Deutsches Tanzarchiv Kölm, © VG BildKunst Bonn.*

Susanne Linke in her reconstruction of Hoyer's dance, a section of Linke's fuller work *Affecte* (1987), her tribute to Hoyer, the last of the original German expressionist dancers and one of Linke's teachers. *Photograph © Ridha Zouari.*

ence directly, her eyes become hollow sockets. Under the light-ing and the cap, her face turns to bone. *Liebe* comes at the end of Hoyer's suite of dances—moody, gothic, and chilly. Insistently inelegant, each mood is underscored by Dimitri Wiatowitsch's music. As she ends this section, Linke sits disconsolate in her hand dance, signaling self-doubt and disintegration.

Inspired by Hoyer's *Liebe*, Linke's own choreography on *Liebe* is a duet for herself and Dietrich that culminates the entire concert cycle of *Affecte*. It is more contemporary in its layering of images and urbane pacing. Here she and Dietrich approach the audience hand in hand through the stage center, then fall down together, buffeted by outside influences. Their movement, full of the same care and pain as Hoyer's, is not so carefully sculpted. The lovers are thrown, sometimes on top of each other, sometimes apart. The perpetual-ongoingness of their journey is punctuated by sud-den full stops that crumple and fall. There is muffled gunfire in the distance. Sometimes the movement explodes with bodies dropping and holding together, then rolling across each other. There is passion and injury in it mixed with shapes of death that integrate briefly then drain of all life.

The end is heroic and at the same time withheld, as the lovers' rolling together becomes less fitful, smooth, and relieved—and the musical collage of trumpets, guns, and compulsive counting turns to Bach's *Cum Sancto Spiritu.* The duet lifts from the floor, the couple wrap themselves in matching robes, plain formal Japanese kimono. They tie their waists, commencing a running in place to-ward the audience. As the run accelerates, Dietrich begins to

Susanne Linke in her neo-expressionist interpretation of Hoyer's themes. Linke stands on one leg with both elbows drawn to the back as she pitches downward in a position of tension and frustration at the beginning of the duet. The kimono she will wear at the end hangs in the background. *Photograph © Ridha Zouari*.

pull ahead of Linke, but her pace continues undaunted, and the blackout ending cuts into the race as it continues to speed and the chorus swells.

The emotional landscape of this work is not so clearly demarcated as Hoyer's. *Affecte* functions as a single whole with emotional accumulations and accelerations over time. As the dance speeds in *Liebe*, the lovers fall repeatedly, then pick themselves up to begin over again. When they are most weary at the end, they put on their kimonos and summon strength to commence the running. Linke treats the emotional landscape in terms of relationship and raw courage and in the contemporary split-second pace of a sometimes tender, often violent, contact choreography.

Certainly we see the human foibles and limitations shared by both partners in *Affecte (Liebe)*. It is the frustrations and strivings of woman, however, that Linke's dances express most clearly. If Linke is behind in the race, she nevertheless states a perspective, throwing her gaze to the horizon as the stage lights darken. The race is not in the winning, she seems to say; in the running itself there is freedom.

Toru Iwashita in Tokyo

May 14, 1990

Toru Iwashita premiered his intimate Butoh work *Liebe* on May 11 at Studio 200, a theater in Ikebukuro in Tokyo. Iwashita's dance is in a solo form typical of Butoh and German expressionism. He uses only the first few feet of stage space, limited by a black-draped back wall extending the width of the stage. This brings his dance to the front, palpably close to the audience.

He casts his dance against Japanese karaoke music, the popular pastime in Japan of singing into a mike along with orchestral recordings of popular songs, Japanese, European, and American.

"Love is touch, touch is love, love is needing to be loved," the sentimental song croons in the interstices of Iwashita's agonistic dance. The music bounces predictably along the surface while Iwashita twists and writhes underneath. In the distance between the banality of the music and the bleating of the dance opens a hope or longing for some new condition, an escape from the boundaries of the walled-in space of the dance and the endless sing-along surface music.

There is nothing special in Iwashita's costume. His clothes are postmodern casual, black pants and white shirt. So the high-pitched theatrics that cloak much of Butoh, particularly the spectacular Dairakudakan company, are absent.

The dance seems wrung from memory, an anguished residue. Often Iwashita uses his hands to enclose the space around his head, as though remembering some echo. Sometimes he actually touches his head, ears, or face, collapsing to the floor, or being flung back against the wall, pinned there for a few frozen seconds, then sliding down in a faint.

At other times pools of light dot the floor across the stage front. Iwashita crawls, reaches, and rolls into and out of the light. His pain is aesthetically deconstructed—we see only parts of it when the light catches slices of his ongoing desperation.

Having burned himself out, Iwashita finally stands up tenu-

Toru Iwashita twists and reaches, looking upward in his danced collaboration with Asuka Kaneko at Ashi Square A in Tokyo. *Photograph © Takashi Yamanaka.*

A spiritual yearn-
ing passes through
Iwashita in his
collaboration
with Asuka
Kaneko. This is
most apparent in
his upward gaze
and the spreading
gesture of his
right hand as the
left hand cups the
movement *gestalt*
from behind.
*Photograph © Takashi
Yamanaka.*

ously. At first it seems his legs might not hold him. Gradually he moves toward a quiet composure, and the cathartic transformation so typical of Butoh endings comes.

The dance cools and ascends in a few silent steps as his face in its fullness receives the light. His arms lift slowly, and the frantic traversing of the wall clings to him, like his sweat-drenched shirt:

> broken wings
> flung to the wall
> *liebestraum*, ice and ash.

Beginner's

Body

Beginner's Body
(Born kindness
is everlasting)

The dance is the space between you and the floor.

Yoko Ashikawa

May 20, 1991

Last night I danced in the Butoh work-shop of Yoko Ashikawa. Kayo Mikami led me through some quiet back streets of Tokyo to Ashikawa's studio. (Yes, there are still a few quiet streets here.) I had become so immune to the Tokyo noise that the sudden lack of it woke me up. Mikami, a graduate student at

Ochanomizu University where I was guest teaching, was becoming my friend. She had studied with the founder and spiritual teacher of Butoh, Tatsumi Hijikata, for several years and was working on a book on Butoh. (As I revise this entry in 1994, Mikami's book, *The Body as Vessel: Tatsumi Hijikata—An Approach to the Techniques of Ankoku-Butoh*,[1] has just been published in Japan. Her book is the first to consider Butoh from the position of an insider—including her experience with Hijikata and, more importantly, the first appearance of notes from rehearsals that capture the distinct methods of the original Butoh.)

Yoko Ashikawa was an even earlier student of Hijikata. After his death in 1986, she began to infuse Hijikata's methods of teaching and choreography with her own. In 1991 she was still teaching, but since then members of Hocutobo dance company have been developing her Butoh teaching method and practicing the communal lifestyle she inherited from Hijikata. In the shared work of Butoh, the Japanese tradition of group harmony is valued over Western individualism by Hocutobo, where no one is featured as a star performer. Mikami explained to me that Hijikata had originated the basic techniques of Butoh, while his partner Kazuo Ohno was noted for the elegance of his performing style and the improvisational essence of Butoh.

Mikami talked to me of Hijikata much in the same manner that Natsu Nakajima had on my first visit to Japan. They loved Hijikata, they said, because he loved them. Each person was important to him. He taught Butoh as a way of life—of being fully alive in present time. "Butoh is now, always now," is how Mikami put it.

Ashikawa's studio was inconceivably small as a dance space, two rooms in a modest Japanese house. The rooms had been cleared, the floors were wood and felt good on my bare feet. Ashikawa began by talking with the students, much as Ohno had in the class I observed him teach years before. There were about twenty-five students there. Maybe half were foreigners: Europeans and Americans. A young man from the University of North Carolina at Greensboro, a young woman from Switzerland, and a Japanese student all whispered their translations of Ashikawa's lesson in my ear. In fact the translations continued throughout the class and became increasingly more audible as time went on. During the class performances at the end, the bilingual element of the class entered into the poetry. Students spontaneously added their verbal interpretation of the movement imagery to Ashikawa's original poetic text that served as improvisational motivation.

Ashikawa's remarks at the beginning were also spun out poetically, intuitively, like Zen when it aims to disrupt logic. "Start from the viewpoint that you are handicapped," she advised in terms of dancing. For me this means adopting the existential attitude of "not knowing," to be open to whatever comes, or attaining what is called in Zen a "beginner's mind." As Shunryu Suzuki puts it: "In the beginner's mind there are many possibilities, but in the mind of the expert, there are few." "Beginner's mind," *shoshin*, was a favorite expression of Dogen-zenji. It expresses the Zen way of making calligraphy also, not trying to make something beautiful or skillful, just giving full attention as if discovering writing (or any action) for the first time.[2] One's original nature is renewed in the discovery, and effortless freedom of action can be realized. Ashikawa talked about freedom in terms of change and constancy in nature. "In nature things seem different everyday. What we see is constantly changing, but the conditions for change are regular," she told us. Then she spoke of change as the condition of dance. "Dance has its roots in our flesh," she said, "deeply entwined with intuitions and the free play of our emotions, transfiguring the body."

She taught that Butoh grows out of felt imagery, and that internalizing the idea or image is the difficult part, because you must get rid of the conscious effort of visualizing before you can internalize. She added that the audience for Butoh might not receive the exact image the dancer internalizes, but they cannot mistake the imagistic process. The process of imaging for both the dancer and the audience is at the aesthetic core of Butoh. "Butoh accepts that fiction is another kind of reality," she said. "Should you be able to really visualize an enormous eye looking at you from behind?" she asked. "The answer is basically 'Yes.'"

In the dimly lit small rooms, the workshop was like a salon gathering of artists. After Ashikawa had expressed her thoughts on Butoh, she introduced the Japanese critic, Nario Goda, who sat with us on the floor and talked further of Butoh, especially how he related it to Greek tragedy and the idea of "eternal return" in Greek thought and the philosophy of Nietzsche. "Something like you and me will in the process of time occur again," he said. Rational thought does not propel Butoh; it lies behind thought in the cycling and recycling of our emotions and the knowledge of

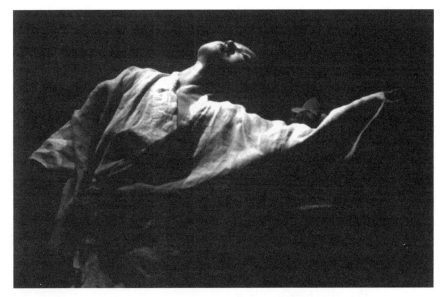

Kayo Mikami, Butoh dancer and scholar, in her concert-length dance cycle *Kenka* (Consecration of Flowers, 1992). *Photograph by Andre Chambat.*

our body. Butoh starts from the body in the moment, not from a script.

Goda criticized modern dance and also contemporary theater, which proceeds from reason and depends on theatrical devices and manipulations including the large Butoh company Dairakudakan in its focus on spectacle. He expanded on Ashikawa's statement of getting rid of concepts emphasizing the kinaesthetic feeling behind them. "If you want to know what wood is like, tap on it. Tap on bone to know bone, and tap on your body likewise to find out what it is."

Ashikawa asked a student about his experience of doing *hoko* or *hokohtai*, the basic Butoh walk. He answered that he felt he was floating, like a ghost above the earth. Then we stood up to begin the walk, which Ashikawa motivated with poetic imagery in the manner of her teacher Hijikata.

. . . Smoke is coming out
from all your joints
There is a big plate of
water on your head and
razor blades under your
feet

Your eyes are open, but
they don't see anything,
There is a big eye in
the middle of your forehead
that mirrors a distant
landscape

Strings are attached to
your joints, you float
above the earth, not
moving yourself

Your spirit goes before
you—form follows
behind

Your sides are pieces
of your body moving out
into space

The walk proceeds like the slow smooth pace of Noh theater
but more in the manner of a smoky dream. The plate of water on
the head lowers the body's center of gravity, the knees bend
softly and slightly, opposing the attenuated lightness of the ballet aesthetic, which floats like a balloon—up, up, and away from
the earth. Butoh can also be light, but its center of gravity is low
and connected to the earth. Butoh lightness is akin to emptiness
and ease and is friendly to gravity.

Ashikawa began a variation on *hokohtai*, further developing the
imagery. This was performed by the women:

. . . smoke is moving up from your
feet, flowing upward like incense
a light strikes the
face from above

now the hair floats
back on a river . . . the hair floats
up in the wind . . .

The walk was further stylized by the men, the imagery becoming more choreographed but allowing for each dancer's own
body dynamic, as Ashikawa described:

There is a black hole
in your thigh . . .
a hole in your chest

From the palm of your
hand, a fish is
swimming up your arm

You stink of fish

You can watch your own
eyes from the back of your head,
see your own brain

Your back is wet and dirty
crawling with stench

You walk from north to south
but your feet do not
do the walking
your eyes walk

The sun moves from east to west,
your eyes become magnetized
by a comet
appearing in the east
moving across the sky

As the men inch slowly forward (indicating the direction of north to south), their knees are soft, their eyes vibrating and moving up into the skull, and a nauseous aura clumps them together. Ashikawa reaches up with her drum in front of them, high to the right corner of their walking direction, and taps continuously, moving across the form of the clumped dancers to the left side of the room as she positions the direction of the comet. They follow the tapping with their inverted gaze, the head rotating smoothly to the left against the forward motivation of the walk and the upward crawling stench of fish. The spaced directions of the movement becomes choreographed as a result of the imagery. Finally an image of some diabolical creature materializes in front of the dancers, crowding them backward, pushing them more inside themselves, shrinking the movement.

As two groups of men performed the images, they became choreographically shaped in clear spacial orientations and blended feeling tones. Each man's revelation of the imagery compounded the whole. A similarly choreographed phrase for women was developed from Ashikawa's image of a peacock walking on the diagonal line of the room with the eyes and face looking askance on the opposing diagonal:

There are antenna
on your head

You have a big tail
behind you and
are wearing high-heeled shoes

Your fingers are soft feathers
As you change your direction
to the opposite
diagonal, the gaze changes
across diagonals, and
there is a cloud of rain
above you
Go away from the cloud
go down into the dust
and backwards being
pulled by your
right side

Then the women worked on a dream variation of the peacock theme:

Your head rests on
your right hand
leaning toward the
right shoulder

(Each woman found her own resting spot for the head; some cupped the right elbow with the left hand to support the right arm as a pillow for the head.)

I condensed Ashikawa's imagery into two seventeen-syllable haiku in the classic form of five, seven, five:

Dreams in the guest room
on the dining room table . . .
the peacock wakes up

Desert Waterfall
I wake up on my sofa . . .
a garden inside

The last section of the class was freely improvised by both men and woman on poetry that began with a giant ear. Thus, Ashikawa jokingly called this set of improvisations *King Ear*.

I developed short haiku from her movement images. As spontaneously improvised, three-line haiku can be shorter or longer than the usual form of seventeen syllables. In English they are often even shorter because our syllables have longer sounds than the typical two-letter syllables of Japanese. Like calligraphy, the way of haiku is based on simplicity and a beginner's mind. Thus haiku poetry is not just a matter for professional poets but more of a folk and Zen art. Anyone can make haiku poems, since they are not nearly so much about mastery or finding the right word as they are about noticing nature, and their content shakes hands with daily life as well. Zen haiku often detail seasonal changes and are especially serene, but paradoxically, they can challenge perception and stimulate reflection.

My haiku focus on first impressions of performing Ashikawa's improvisations, my beginner's body, and Butoh's return to the body as a part of nature.

KING EAR HAIKU

mixing flesh and floor
one big ear
forgetting its body

partly inside its mother
Oh! the newborn
animal emerges

Stone Still Body
There is nothing
That is not moving

Rolling together
groin and gut; if the stone breaks
yaaa, what will happen?

Haiku can be a pleasurable exercise in remembering otherwise
forgotten details in an unmistakable form. The master of haiku,
Basho, who died in 1694, influenced the economy and simplicity
of this very Japanese art. A year before his death Basho wrote:

chrysanthemums bloom
in a gap between stones
of a stonecutter's yard.

Tree

Tree
(Rite of wood)

June 2, 1990

Eating goat's cheese from his farm
with Min Tanaka
I drink sake!

Last night after the performance of *Tree IV Installation* at Plan B in Tokyo, several of us sat around a table with Min Tanaka, while others conversed around the room, sometimes joining in at our table where food was being served. Eggs from Tanaka's farm were on sale. There was plenty of green tea and sake. Tanaka was friendly in a quiet way. I remember his broad pleasant face and that he liked to talk about his work when drawn out in conversation.

We talked in general of Butoh and dance. Nario Goda, the Butoh critic, was there even though he had injured his foot on the way to the performance. It was obvious that Butoh had occupied his writing and thinking for many years. His language was lively, and I needed an interpreter to understand both him and Tanaka. Two of my friends helped out. One, Chio Kawaguchi, had been Tanaka's dance teacher when he was studying at Tsukuba University. The other was my Zen teacher's daughter, Akiko Akane. This was Akiko's first Butoh concert. I thought she might not like it, but she slipped easily into the aesthetic, perhaps through her association with Zen, her teaching of yoga, and her poetic imagination. We talked in particular about *Tree IV*. Tanaka's intention in *Tree IV* was not a literal one. He was not necessarily referring to nature; rather, it was about "family," he said, and "race." I told him I understood the symbolism in my own language, in the expression *family tree*, tracing and picturing genealogy.

Chio Kawaguchi, who introduced me to Tanaka, remembered when he got arrested for dancing nude in the gym at Tsukuba. I said, "Oh, he got arrested?" She answered "Yes," emphatically, her eyes growing wider: "Many times!" She left little doubt concerning Tanaka's determination to pursue his aesthetic conscience. Now she could smile about it, but I wondered (and hardly dared ask) what university colleagues and officials must have thought about it at the time. This would not go down well in American gymnasia (though I remember some nudity in our own gym dur-

Min Tanaka in *I Sit*. Photograph © Kevin Bubriski.

ing the 1960s) and Japan is more conservative. Tonight's concert was not nude, but it was bare. Tanaka's Butoh is both similar and different from other Butoh I have seen. It is true to the concern Butoh artists have had for Japanese identity, and like other Butoh, its existential question, who am I? also universalizes. It moves the audience, East and West, to questions of human identity through its development of the body's many shades or states of being. Unlike other Butoh, its theatrics are not spectacular (like Dairakudakan and Sankai Juku), and the ending is not a total catharsis, only a momentary resolution of human travail.

Tanaka's style is matter-of-fact. Whereas much Butoh makes use of dramatic transformation through facial expression (especially Yoko Ashikawa and Natsu Nakajima), Tanaka presents the face in a straightforward manner. Faces are not without expression, but neither is facial gesture cultivated. The face is let alone to reflect each person's singularity. I found myself studying faces as part of the aesthetic of his work, particularly when the dancers would sit facing the audience.

In the small theater, seating about fifty, we could almost touch the dancers. The dancers did not look at us, nor did they look into a beyond. They just sat, almost as one of us, without projecting —their eyes like windows receiving light, their faces deeply quiet. The dancers could sit comfortably at the edge of the small elevated box stage with their feet touching the floor. They could move in front of it and could enter from crouching behind the stage. Their heads appeared first, lingering there in sight before fully emerging.

The dance is a study in perspective, with dancers elevated on the box, some dancing a distance behind it, and some near the walls beside it. Others move momentarily in front of the box and close to the audience. They also appear and vanish between rice paper screens at the side, as though moving in and out of a small traditional house.

The dancers wear tattered clothing in somber colors and are often dimly lit. There is habit in their gestures, especially as they move close to the earth in squats and crouches. There is sometimes resignation and emptiness, and at other times this lassitude turns to conflicted movement. Agitated shapes evolve slowly, gray and hiding, floating, flailing, softly falling. The Japanese expression *yasashiku yawarakaku* (softly and gently) bespeaks the tender character of the movement.

When the men are standing at full height on the box, their faces are covered by a hanging flat of wood. A noise flutters in the background. In front of the box, two dancers embrace—stiffly, tenuously—like old scarecrows. The men eventually move down to uncover their faces and sit in a quiet circle as a woman performs twitching gestures, repeating her daily work. Events overlap. Two men in a corner struggle in a half-conscious dream state.

Folded in half with her torso hanging from the hip joints and moving on all fours, a primate dancer travels carefully, slowly, skirting the entire edge of the box. The music swells, then ends abruptly. The dancers remain sitting together. Their eyes are open. They neither stare nor smile. They simply see and are silent together, yet each one is alone. We sit silently with them for a long time. In the waiting, patience. In tomorrow, yesterday and today.

I wrote four haiku on the dance, then decided to tie them together.

LINKED HAIKU ON TREE IV

Agitated shapes evolve slowly:

grey, hiding
floating, flailing
softly falling, dead leaves . . .

yasashiku yawarakaku

noise flutters
old scarecrows embrace
one head then two . . .

yasashiku yawarakaku

The dancers remain:

family tree *ya*,
sitting circle *so desuka*,
alone together each one . . .

yasashiku yawarakaku

in memory
shapes held and faint
begin again tomorrow . . .

yasashiku yawarakaku

Amazing Grace

Kazuo Ohno's Performance in Yokohama

Grace
(Kindness of grass)

June 11, 1990

Not all Butoh is equal to me. I would rather watch Kazuo Ohno dance than any other male soloist I can think of, including Baryshnikov and Fred Astaire. Ohno laughed when (in a sudden burst of hero worship) I told him this at a concert of Isle, Laughing Stone Dance Theater. I was surprised to see the great Mr. O standing alone and unrecognized in the hallway at the intermission of Isle's SPACE PART 3 later this month. I don't know if Ohno recognized me from his workshops, but he treated me with the same grandfatherly warmth that I had experienced in his studio. I have noticed how comfortable people feel around Ohno, and I want to be more like him. He never seems to be in a hurry but takes time to talk and listen. Ohno holds the whole world in his hands, and time itself makes his dances beautiful.

Like the popular and commercial Baryshnikov and Astaire, Ohno also has the gift of grace, and the gift to entertain, but more than they, he gives us much to think about. In Ohno, we can see ourselves, our human fragility, transitory hopefulness, and contradictions. His body is full of conscience and abandon. He celebrates and grieves, embodying a human condition and evoking the mystery of the body. He universalizes.

He amazes. Ohno has an ability to include a multinational audience in his conjured states. He distances his dance stylistically in an unfamiliar mixture of cultures, historical periods, and highly idiosyncratic costumes. Then he crosses the distance to become one with the audience, as he makes their human failings and ecstasies his own. Certainly I project myself into the dance as I identify the qualities I value in Ohno's dancing. For me this is a reason to be an audience.

Ohno was eighty-four years old when I saw him perform his work *Suiren* (or *Waterlily*, premiered in 1987) in Yokohama. His age is noted by the audience; it has become part of his aesthetic. He is at once young and old, male and female, one moment elegant and fresh as a flower and the next spent and withered. He transforms temper and character throughout the work, and I change with him as he crosses time and reverses gender.

Kazuo Ohno in *Suiren* (*Waterlily*) premiered in Yokohama in 1987.
Photograph by Naoya Ikegami.

Ohno's son Yoshito, his partner in the dance, transforms also, but not across generations so much as within himself. In *Suiren*, Yoshito evolves deathlike from a gray-suited, bent figure (perhaps a man on the subway) toward a contained and peaceful figure at the closing of the work. Tense and jerky shapes mark the cataleptic nature of his first solo.

Against Yoshito's jolting dance, Ohno appears first as an elegant old woman carrying a parasol. His eyes are liquid containers filled with tragedy and mystery. Like the lace of his dress, his wrists and fingers can be delicate and vulnerable, wintry and aloof, then sensitive and consoling.

As Ohno leaves the space in shadowed light, Yoshito's gray-suited death figure comes to life, he folds softly, then untangles his body. From a crouch, he grows an upward-leading zig-zag claw. His movement bursts, then settles decisively. These sharp spurts of compact, whole-body motion bite against the sounds of blowing wind and the music of Pink Floyd. His poses are catatonic and stiff, continuing into the darkness at the edges of the lighted space.

Ohno reenters gently with the sound of thunder, trailing a long yellow kimono and leaning on a staff. Like haiku, he moves very simply. His face implores as his neck lengthens. He beckons to the distance, and the audience follows intently. He is alternately happy and tired, but never grotesque. His manner is exploratory and inquisitive. He becomes a child with a flower. His almost naked body is exposed as the kimono loosens. Gestures dissolve and reappear: self-embracing, squatting, striving to see, crawling, quiet. Ohno never drops me—even in the detailed slowness and introspection.

Eventually Ohno effects a more lusty appearance, dancing in a masculine black suit and white shirt. Even so, he looks like a beautiful woman—maybe a mannish Lauren Bacall with her strong angular face and warm-blooded gestures. As the dance nears closure to the strains of Bach and Handel, Yoshito transforms from a gray man into a white lotus goddess, while Ohno has evolved from feminine lace to a tailored and robust figure. Throughout, transformations guide the dance, like changings of nature, distilled for momentary notice. Human malleability is at the heart of the dance.

Many choreographers hope to inspire interpretations of their work that move beyond or expand upon their intent, and Ohno is no exception. When I spoke to him about *Waterlily* in a class I took from him early in July, he said Monet's painting influenced him. In order to avoid explaining the dance, he spoke of "taking care of life," a consistent theme with Ohno. He also spoke of a "ghost coach," and I was reminded that ghosts are also common in Kabuki and Noh. Ohno told me that nature, as explored in his recent work, *Ka Cho Fu Getsu* (1990), is his guide—"flowers and wind, moon and birds." My haiku on *Suiren* keeps changing. Now (July 11, 1997) it remembers Ohno's hands:

> How lonely how long
> the grey branch dreams a body
> of lotus petals

Hot

Spring

In Hakone Yumoto

Onsen, Hot Spring
(Bathing
your body
and heart)

June 23, 1990

Dead dragonflies bathe
in morning mist our whispers
through the bamboo fence

The author's snapshot of a fish pond with reflections
of the mountains, taken during her stay at a traditional hot spring hotel (*ryokan*) in Hakone.

The

Waters

of

Life

Waters of Life
(Morning clouds
and
flowing water)

July 4, 1990

After seeing Ohno dance *Waterlily* this
year, I visited his studio in Yokohama
again with Akiko Akane and my friend
from America, Juliett Crump. Akiko
translated for us. We talked to Ohno
and danced in his thematic improvisation class on the mother's feeding of
the universe to her growing child.

"Tonight we start in the mother's
womb," Ohno said:

We are swimming in her waters, and
drinking her life. When you move you

should touch something, hear your mother, touch her. Keep this in mind—your body yourself is your mother. She is feeding you the universe as it exists in everything, even so small a creature as a moth. The form of the universe imprints a moth wing. The mother contains the universe, she makes a soup of the universe to feed her baby, a soup of the moth's wing.

As I moved I remembered my own child moving and growing inside me, and as I touched the memory of my rounded soft belly, I knew myself inside my own mother. Everything seemed as it should be. I felt no need to move further, and finished in a rounded shape.

Kazuo Ohno and his son Yoshito Ohno. *Photograph* © *Kevin Bubriski.*

How I Got the Name "Bright Road Friend"

With
Zen
Teacher
Shodo
Akane
in
Tsuchiura

Bright,
oh Bright,
oh Bright
(Bright,
bright,
bright)

July 5, 1990

Akiko Akane took me to Tsuchiura outside of Tokyo to meet her family. Akiko
is the yoga teacher I met here in Tokyo
at "Hatagaya Mansion," as we like to
refer to our noisy apartment complex
next to the freeway in Hatagaya. I was
on leave from my university to be a vis-
iting professor in dance at Ochanomizu
University and to research Butoh, the
Japanese avant garde movement in theater known as "the dance of darkness."
I was drawn to the metaphysical qualities of Butoh in its trust of the uncon-

身
心
一
如

Sondra Fraleigh serving tea. Calligraphy: "Body and Mind Are One."
Photograph by Jim Dusen.

scious. I also had secret hopes that I might be able to meditate in Zen temples, that I might find a Zen teacher, but I did not know how to go about this. As fate would have it, Akiko began to talk to me one day while I was waiting for the elevator at Hatagaya Mansion. Now I was on my way to meet Akiko's father Shodo Akane, Zen author and teacher (sensei).

I had bought a tea set for the Akanes in Kobe City on the coast. We became friends immediately, as though we already knew each other. Akane-sensei and I began sharing haiku after I told him my haiku definition of dance, one that had come to me at the end of my dancing in a Butoh workshop with Yoko Ashikawa in Tokyo:

> Stone still body
> there is nothing
> that is not moving

"Same mind," Akane-sensei pronounced in his understanding of my mind through the poem. This was to me an odd and entirely fresh statement of what we generally call "a meeting of minds." Then he brought out his own haiku, beautifully written in calligraphy, many, many of them. Mrs. Akane and Akiko were amazed. They had not seen his poems. Sensei gave me three of his books, which have been translated into English, rich with bold calligraphy. In the back of one he wrote these words: "Every day be beautiful." Its broader meaning is: "Every day find peace." This simple message still jars me loose from life's complexities and always gives me pause for renewal.

Mrs. Akane danced for us that day. It was my favorite performance in Japan, since I love to see the heartfelt dance of ordinary people, celebrating each other in the moment. She danced in samurai robes, a dance usually done by men. Akiko's grandfather sang while she danced—a song about Fuji mountain. (Fuji is considered to be a god in Japan.) After the dance, I was asked if I would also dance for the family gathering, but I hesitated, explaining that I had no special costume or music. But sensei insisted and said that grandfather could sing Fuji mountain again. As my excuses were running out, sensei became firm: "Just Dance *mu*," he said. (Or, as Akiko translated: "Empty yourself and dance.") *Mu* is a Zen term for emptiness, and his statement cleared my mind. So I prepared with a few moments of silence, then began to improvise from scratch, not knowing the words to grandfather's song and without a plan. I let grandfather's voice fill me up, and the movement felt good. There was sweetness and peace in the slow pace of it. I let myself go into the radiance of the visit to mark the occasion with my dance to grandfather's singing of *Mt. Fuji*.

When I finished, grandfather vowed that we should embark on a world tour together as a song and dance team. Sensei responded with the shortest five-syllable haiku:

Bright
        oh bright
                oh bright

He gave me the name of "Bright Road Friend." He says my name means, "bringing together all beings in learning." Now, years later, I feel more than ever the obligation of such a name. I certainly drop the "all." He intended, I believe, to point out the importance of the teacher's path. In America, we need to learn how to honor our teachers. Then maybe we will honor more the path of learning. When I am invited to bring American dancers to perform in Japan, when I come to teach, or when I write about the meaning I find in Butoh, I examine my name, the elegance of friendship, and my experience of meeting the Akane family.

At the close of the day Mrs. Akane performed the tea ceremony for us in their tea room. It was a revelation to me in its weightless simplicity. As we were served, we were included in the slow smooth time of her ritualized movements. It was like a silent group meditation, a floating in time. Then Mrs. Akane gave me presents of her home-crafted jewelry, a further sharing of talent. The colors and sounds of the day danced between us in the quiet ceremony of tea and presents. It was so fulfilling to finish without talk, to respect the senses of sight, taste, smell, and touch in the feel of the large earthen bowls and frothy green tea.

As evening came, we sat in sensei's meditation room. The only object in the room was a concentric nest of black lacquer bowls given to him by his teacher. When we said good-bye after a stroll in his garden, he answered my questions. "Zen is nature," sensei said simply, placing a tiny red flower in my buttonhole.

The

Existential

Answer

Interview
with
Butoh
Critic
Nario
Goda
in
Tokyo

Darkness
(Ink-bars
contain
thousands
of colors)

Our land is as small as the cat's forehead.

Nario Goda

July 9, 1990

Fraleigh: What is Japanese about Butoh?

Goda: I'm Japanese, so it is difficult to dissociate enough to say.

Fraleigh: Could you speak then about the difference between Noh and Butoh?

Goda: Noh has a long history, including a sense of time that is native to

Tatsumi Hijikata sitting on a fence. From Eikoh Hosoe's photography book on Hijikata and his performance of *Komaitachi* (1969).

Noh. Butoh has only thirty years of history. A particular intention is apparent in Butoh. Its slowness is more intentional/ artificial than Noh. Butoh is an international mix of elements, from its principle: what is existence, what is body? *The body is the link.*

In principle, there are no differences between one body and the body of everyone. But there are differences in the way we dance.

Ballet is six inches above the floor, Butoh is six inches below the floor. This is a way of saying that visually the body in Butoh is lower than in Western dances influenced by ballet. Not many Westerners can do the Japanese squat. This manner of lowering the body is also different on and off stage. A stage squat is centered, while an ordinary squat is bent like bowing.

Our land is as small as the cat's forehead. The onstage effect of this squatting is reconcentrating our existence, making it fuzzy —ghostly, under the willow tree. Sometimes it seems that the body has no legs, or that it is always woman. Why do we have to pursue these squatting and ghostly postures then? In pursuing yin and yang, shadow and light, space and form, Butoh doesn't treat sides equally. It tries to picture the shadows and express real life.

Fraleigh: What is the place of light in Butoh?

Goda: There is the philosophy that postwar Japan is always looking on the bright side, but Butoh is looking at agony and conflict. It is closer to the existence of the Japanese in the aftermath of war. Butoh founder Tatsumi Hijikata worked in the miserable aftermath of war. He had an unfortunate family life. He had ten brothers and sisters, of which he was the youngest. His sister was sold into prostitution (because his parents were poor). In 1934 there was a bad famine, his sister went to Southeast Asia to earn money. She suffered like his mother; so Hijikata became a revolutionary.

His work is Japanese dadaism, and he associates with ideas close to a pure communism. Also at the root of Butoh is *Kinjiki*, which literally means forbidden color. It is a reference to forbidden sex or homosexuality. It starts in Butoh from Hijikata and is the title of a book by Mishima. The content of *Kinjiki* (1959) is also strongly affected by Jean Genet. Japan was highly political after the war and the Japan-U.S. security pact was accepted by the general public, but revolution was not uniformly welcome. Hijikata's reactionary work was rejected by dance criticism at first, but Mishima supported Hijikata.

Kinjiki was the first Butoh. It perceived homosexuality positively. Its eroticism shows a relation between humans, but with no differences between men and women in some senses. What is erotic does not depend on sex. The erotic is eternal and limitless.

In Hijikata's dance, *The Rebellion of the Body*, the hand is killed, but from Butoh logic the killing is . . . the whole persona. It expresses a paradoxical and revolutionary love. Clubbing, for instance, is more personal and shows more affection than shooting or dropping bombs.

There are two things the dark side can give us: You can see the reflection of the bright by looking at the dark, and you can sense tiny things easier. If you are poor you have more time to see the sunset or the green of leaves. In complete darkness you can see a tiny light. This is the basis of Butoh. If you gain more and more experience in dance, you begin to realize not only light—but a dark conscience. Butoh became popular through these ideas.

When you look at Min Tanaka, the color is gray and black. Hijikata used pink kimono and underwear. The lighting effect on stage is gorgeous; the color is simple. In our ordinary sense the color pink is associated with the prostitute. This color can become aesthetic with lighting effects. This color, long held in contempt, can also turn beautiful.

Fraleigh: How does today's Butoh relate to the original Butoh?

Goda: To feel one's body is highly individualistic. Hijikata laid down Butoh principles. His movement, sometimes elegant, austere, or lonely, was unpredictable. A Butoh method developed, but the experience is individual. A basic attitude or approach is common in Butoh, both past and present, but expression varies. One attitude remains central to Butoh, however; the reaction of the body—it answers the world outside.

Fraleigh: What is your opinion of the very popular Butoh company Sankai Juku?

Goda: Some journalists say they are post-Butoh—they are a boundary. I think the Sankai Juku is expressing visual patterns of existential beginnings, using the body as material. Within your body consciousness, sometimes there is a subconscious rebellion you cannot explain. If you pursue these strange things, you show your confused self, and you feel the shock of your body. It is different to understand by the brain than to perceive by the senses.

Resonance between the performer and the audience is without total understanding of the brain.

For myself, I don't like Sankai Juku. They give too much; there is no room for the audience to play. In Hijikata's Butoh, half of the self is not conceived, so it is very dynamic. It is theatrical because it is alive and unfinished. In this way, the audience can read it freely. Total art is totalizing (totalitarian). We can learn to be happy with what is unfinished and imperfect.

Hocutobo performances by Ashikawa used rhythmic music sometimes, but when the dancer is with the rhythm, it is thin. When the dance is off the rhythm, you can selectively perceive the whole in the gaps.

Fraleigh: Your criticism lent understanding to Butoh throughout its developing years when it was largely rejected in Japan as psychedelic, odd, dirty, and spastic. You deciphered Butoh's messages. What about today? Does Butoh have a future?

Goda: We can try to foresee our future in a real life sense, but we don't even know when we will die. The existential answer is that we can't know our future; this is the essence of Butoh expression. If you perform what you experience, if you show your confused self, it is total. Look at Butoh today, it is diverse and confused. That is Butoh. A knight on a white horse may appear to rescue this confusion, but would we recognize such dance as Butoh?

Hokohtai, the Walking Body

Hokohtai,
the Walking Body
(Feeling free
in movement)

October 22, 1992

Hokohtai, the impersonal (universalized) "walking body," is at the root of Butoh. Its grace arises through method in purifying motion of intention, getting rid of or emptying the self. When I perform this Butoh walk, I experience a meditative movement manner of entering the Zen question: What is *mu*? (What is emptiness?).

I most understand *mu* aesthetically in the dancing *hokohtai* of Yoko Ashikawa. In *Nagareru Kubi* (Floating Visage,

New York, October 22, 1992), she performs with an emptying or absence near mystical nothingness that erases identity and ego. Anonymous as a dry leaf, she moves without willing, resting on breezes, asleep standing up, borne and dropped to lie along oblique paths. She gives up the dance to the space around her.

As she sometimes states in a confusing manner to confound students in her classes: "The dance is the space between you and the floor." Like Zen, this definition aims to disrupt logic. And it is true that dancing, like Zen, is not about logic. Like Zen, dance is not about doing movement, but more about being moved. Dance is rooted in our flesh and emotions, but when it is in tune with our true nature, it relinquishes these, ultimately. In those moments of emptiness when the dancer is lost in the "I" of the storm, she is not dancing the dance, the dance is dancing her. Then she is "Not-I," not the doer. Butoh has what all dance has that culminates in detachment and the transfiguration of the body.

> Mind and body falling off,
> Falling off is mind and body.[1]

Soto Zen

Akeno Ashikawa and Hakutobo, the Butoh company established by Yoko Ashikawa, one of the female founders of Butoh. *Photograph © Kevin Bubriski.*

Dance and Zen, Kyo Ikiru

With Zen Teacher Shodo Akane in Tokyo

 Kyo Ikiru (Live Today)

Shodo Akane

Kyo Ikiru,
Live Today
(One day
reflects
one life)

November 5, 1992

When I visit Tokyo, I repeat the directions to my *ryokan* in Asakasa so often that they become second nature, or unconsciously a part of me, like a well-rehearsed dance. Now I distill them in the form of haiku:

face temple, go left
under yellow lanterns, left
under turquoise sign

On my last visit in October-November of 1992, my Zen teacher and friend, Shodo Akane, explained Zen to me as "the rhythm of the universe, the rhythm of nature." In this Tokyo anthill of packed-together, noisy villages, my little haiku for finding my way home becomes part of my internal rhythm, my inner dance (my practical Zen dance) compelled by the city rhythms and my own nature.

More and more, I understand life as a dance-in-the-making, a choreography wherein my steps and turns are laying down a traceable ground pattern. They show where I have been, but more importantly, they are the foundation for where I go now—into the moment. This is the aspect of life's dance that Akane-sensei spoke to me about as "being in the middle of the stream." *Time* is the intangible that links dance and Zen. Or more accurately, dance and Zen are of the essence of time and its incomprehensible partner, *timelessness*. While we cannot see or taste time, it is nevertheless of our experience. When we dance (be it spontaneous play, folk steps, ritual enactment, or theater), we can enter a state of consciousness that is like the single-pointed, present-centered consciousness of Zen. We move in the flowing river that Akane-sensei explained to me as timeless, "the endless spirit of Zen."

When we dance, we become more than ourselves. Our skin melts along with our ego, that blind impasse that separates us from our larger nature and each other. Our dancer eyes don't see the object-environment as obstacle, or others as objects. They see inclusively. When we dance, we become kin to the environment and others who are dancers in the stream with us. We lose ourselves (and time as we live it) in the flowing stream. Dance can be defined by this loss. *This is the dancing.*

In many religious mythologies, the dancer represents our god-self capable of transcending the discriminating limits of attachment. In the whirlwind of her motion, the dancer creates and destroys the cosmos. She is both building and burning her steps in the dancing. She is a wildish god who honors her intuition—not looking back or forward—she moves into the eye of the storm. Being fully present, she learns to trust her steps, to erase them in the doing. She does not admire them (self-reflexive awareness signals aesthetic poverty); but she loves her steps in the moment, their piercing time.

American modern dance choreographer Merce Cunningham, who incorporated Zen principles in his work, has used chance procedures to make his dances. He used chance (drawing lots as in a game) in order to detach himself from the choreography or to "get away" from himself, as he said in our dance classes. His was a conscious choice to let go of the authoritarian place of the choreographer in shaping the dance. When I discussed Cunningham's work in its implications for letting go of ego with Japan's choreographer Fumie Kanai, she asked me how I saw the element of the dancer's ego in Japanese modern dance.

I explained that Japanese ballet and modern dancers are so swift and exacting that there is *no time* for dancers to be self-reflexive, or to visualize themselves as in a mirror. In any case, whether the steps are carefully designed or improvised, fast or slow, the (authentic) dance is given up to the storm, allowed to be swept up,

Flower arrangement at Zen temple Zensho-An in Tokyo. *Photographed by the author.*

risking the body, trusting. In the storm there is no time to admire one's steps, only to perform them, to purify intent at the quickening core of consciousness, the dance itself.

Of all the arts, dancing leaves behind so little trace. Its principle purpose is to clear attention, both that of the dancer and those who enter into the spirit of the dance. Dancing purifies the body, animating it through the breath in the wind and fire of rhythmic motion. It wears down the house of the ego, built for self-protection and advancement. Dance is not of the self, neither self-protection nor self-expression, as it is so often called. Rather, dance serves to move one beyond the boundaries of the self toward freedom in the existential and Zen sense: that freedom which liberates the self from the impermanent psyche, releasing thought and action in tune with nature. Zen does not advance, it allows the being of the moment to shine.

Shodo Akane says that in Asia (at least in its core doctrine) "freedom is nature." But how is freedom realized in the nature of the human body? In Paul Ricoeur's existential work *Freedom and Nature* (a study of voluntary and involuntary movement), he teaches that we are engaged in a bodily lived dialectic with nature as we learn our movement. At some point, movement becomes habit, or "second nature."

We can become aware of habit when we pay conscious attention to our movement, and particularly as we acquire skillful movements as in dance, yoga, somatic studies, or ritual. The skills we acquire may also sink back into habit (become second nature), but our awareness has spiraled to a higher level, and in developing conscious attention to our habits, we increase our options for choice. Existentially, this means that we learn how to be choosers, to be alert and not imprisoned by emotion. Eventually this alertness can be manifest in spontaneous response. This is a higher level of freedom than that expressed merely though habit, one that moves us toward enlightenment of the senses, our light and natural body.

The closer we come to realizing our own true nature, the more freedom we realize in our daily lives. But, "what is my true nature?" Or to put it existentially, "who am I?" When I pursue these difficult questions intellectually, I come up against the dead end of thought. These questions cannot be answered by the mind in a straightforward manner. One's true nature can only be experienced according to one's path in life, progressively unfolding in relation to the development of one's talents. We all have natural talents, and we are all natural dancers. Our dance is manifest in those actions we take in tune with our intuition and instinct—aided (but not governed by) intellect. Dance is a paradigm for wholeness and rightness in action, the complete giving of ourselves in a task or endeavor and in our aesthetic expressions as we explore our talents.

Thus gardening and cooking have their own dancing rhythms, as does right action in business and pleasure in conversation or fulfilling friendships when we are carried beyond our ordinary limits of self-expression through our relationships with others. The purpose of Zen is to discover this rhythm, this freedom, as we align with nature (our true selves). In the Zen of dancing, we discover (uncover) our human nature, blessing the "nows" of life, the timeless in the present. In the river, the wind, and the fire, there is surrender (there is dance). There is surrender (there is dance and Zen) in living today. Ultimately there is peace. "Silence is Zen," says Shodo Akane.

Prose

and

Haiku

on

Japan

Green Land
(Green land
and
yellow gold)

July 22–26, 1993

AT THE KABUKI

The anguished hero
        calls for a black kimono
        tinged with light,
        pure patrician purple
        and perfect red,
        bright against
        his white suicide
Wringing past time's trio
        mother and wife
        sit his dilemma

I fashion my rain dance
around these colors.

Still more sharp
    the orange lanterns
        dot the darkness,
            gather the sloping green

       Rain dots my face
    falls in the square pool
    I contemplate alone
    at the Zen temple
      in Shinjuku
      in Tokyo
    in early morning

MORNING RAIN

It has rained for five days straight in Tokyo, and here I am at
Mikawaya Bekkan in my cubicle looking down from my window
into the Japanese garden. For the last two days, I sat in the morning at Toshoji Zen temple in Shinjuku where the entire courtyard
is formed as a pool to catch the rain. Zen-smooth wood floors
surround the pool under an overhang. I sat alone, protected, tun-
ing my attention to the rain, watching the morning lift.

      Rain in July
    the muted morning lifts a
    rainbow from the pool

FROG POND

With golden carp swimming below my window in Asakasa,
I sit once more to enter the day in a pool of rain. Rain is positive in Japan—although the Japanese complain as much about
the inconvenience as anyone.

There is romance in rain.
The slow deep rhythms of the senses move.
Not much to say, even to oneself, when this happens.
                              Thoughts ride the rhythm
                              witnessing the pond as
                              streaming its sounds in play.

Stray, they polish the mind and pass,
as quickly as the mirrored world
reflects the pool.

There is a frog in this pond,
                              green with moss,
                              (Plop! in Asakasa)
                              a big stone frog.

BESIDE MYSELF

today live simply
go with cheerful acceptance
finally, the breeze

All acts have consequence. It begins with small things, simple things. The Chinese keep the middle way. The Japanese let go in cheerful acceptance.

I complain to myself,
all night this noise
at Arima hot springs,
teenage girls with fireworks.

small stuff,
spirals, sparklers, squiggles,
roman candles.

I came for peace.
How could I have known
there would be a
Karaoke bar downstairs?
The travel agent smiled, didn't she?

But the bath is hot,
and clean,
I become simple,
accept cheerfully,
as in Japan.

KUNDALINI

It keeps me company,
no longer

a tingle
     through my left neck and shoulder.

Now it moves me,
beginning slowly (as I came to
Japan),

an oscillation
I can feel between the
          two sides of my head . . .

Well founded, a swaying
        moves my spine like a
snake,
a subtle more expressive total undulation

        from the sitting base, through the low,
middle, upper back;

        then the neck and head. This comfort—
awakening movement—
        reminds me. *I am not the doer.*

Something larger than myself moves
        through me.
Now at fifty-four, I begin to observe, be
        with this . . .

RETURNING TO MIKAWAYA BEKKAN

I looked for the frog pond
out the window of my new room, but only found a concrete
    wall.

Later I looked again
to see a vine with large spreading leaves, two branches

five green leaf-hands
spreading life against the concrete.
Yes, here is wabi-sabi.

And I almost missed it, looking with tired eyes for some
aesthetic less-is-more in my less-is-
small room.
Even the empty earthen bowl
in the alcove didn't
fill the bill
Mono no aware! (of evanescence).
of unostentatiousness.

THE COLOR OF KAMINOYAMA

From my window at
Yumotogosuke Ryokan
in Kaminoyama
near Yamagatta,
the green grows darker

(like mud against putrid orange
antique vases, gathering dust in the market).

Green grows clean
in the twilight.
Twelve bright orange paper lanterns
hang sparely outside
the lonely shape
footing the lush green hill,
like a bit of orange silk
rimming the neck
of a dark dress, underscoring
a twist of long black hair.

HOT SPRING (ONSEN)

I feel you here in my green silence,
eighteen small dishes—
thirty six, or forty-three tidbits
for my palate—a careless count.

Yukuri,
slowly reach across the table.

Yes, I devise this as a form
of conversation.

A self-portrait of author Sondra Fraleigh in a traditional Japanese *yukatta* during a stay at a *ryokan*—a typical hot spring hotel—where the bath is in an outside garden and meals are served in the room.

Speaking with you in absentia
is next to talking to myself—
bathed and wrapped in my yukatta.

Thank you for only criticizing me
three times in twelve years, (then noticing before I did,
and trying so to recant).

It stung my life into lesson . . .
Now the window lacquers,
augers the night, as I remember.

Post-Butoh

Chalk

Footprints
(Buddha's
foot-stone)

October 3, 1993

In *Solo 1*, Annamirl Van der Pluijm weaves unlikely strands of dance with glaring intensity akin to the slow burn of incense. She dances hot and cold, but the intellectual construction of the work in cleanly divided sections leading from one cultural body to another (from elongated Butoh walks to stabbing tangos) gives the whole a decidedly minded character. In fact, we see her mind at work from the outset. Even as the audience enters the carefully prepared black and white space, Van der Pluijm is just com-pleting her chalking of the long rectangular floor leading to the white back wall. The white floor and back wall are framed by the intimate black box theater. There is a single stool waiting near the back; her folded kimono, flamenco shoes, and soft leather boots—a harbinger of the dance to come—laid center front, nearly at our feet.

The dance is many-faceted, or indeed, of several bodies in its extremes. It could have been cut from black and white paper; its edges are so final. There is no fuzz in Van der Pluijm's dancing. Even her eyes slice through the light. And they *see*—not being withdrawn in the once-popular postmodern aversions, nor cast beyond in the mythic realms of historic modern.

There are two major links to Butoh in this work—one is the-atrical, the other inheres in the movement. As in Butoh whiteface, Van der Pluijm plays with light and masking, but she powders the floor instead of her face and uses only black costumes. Like Butoh gestures that coalesce and modulate slowly in glaring light, Van der Pluijm's gestures stand out. Her precision as a dancer make them shine all the more. Unlike the face in Butoh that car-ries so much emotion, Van der Pluijm's face is not gestural, but it is concentrated through the essence of each movement style she explores. The face projects nothing extra; indeed, much of the dance's success lies in its candor—when this is at issue. For in-stance, the modeling poses that could easily dwindle into nar-cissism are reduced through sudden changes of attention that throw the dancer's focus (and ours) away from her body.

Annamirl Van der Pluijm throws her head back and narrows her body in
the center of the chalked floor of *Solo 1*, performed at the festival of new
dance in Montreal in 1993. In the background her kimono (a reference to
butoh) is left on the chair. *Photograph © Michel Pellanders.*

She begins the dance with the other strong allusion to Butoh
in the ceremonial donning of a black kimono and a journey of
painstaking, carefully paced steps, patiently moving away from the
audience the full length of the space to sit on the far stool. This
slow-motion walking is privileged, like the upper-class samurai
in Japan who evolved the slow-moving Noh theater, Japan's equivalent of classical ballet. Yet in this walk, as in Butoh, there is less
of Japan's courtly aristocracy and more of its inscrutable inward-

ness. Van der Pluijm is a remarkable dancer. She performs a sitting flamenco in which her legs from the knees down move in an odd duet, exchanging unisons and contrasts, almost as though they were two dancers instead of two legs. Her subsequent development of a tango to Astor Piazzolla's music languishes in deep twists and whirling turns, tracing baroque curves that mark figures in the center of the chalked floor like ice skating. But even these turgid loops and braids, and the emancipated bluegrass jumps and flings that follow, are restrained within the long white rectangle.

Free is never quite free in this dance, as we are reminded in her final recapitulation of three contracted themes repeated over and over with ever-increasing speed. Repetition, that worn-out minimalist formula, is effective here and also original. Butoh inscrutables, cool mechanical cruelties of modeling, and blazing tangos chase each other in Van der Pluijm's accumulative phrases.

When she breaks and exits the powdered performance, it remains as residue on her dress. Chalk footprints mark her trail from the whitened space onto the clean black floor—each print a reminder of the dance left behind, rounded pads for toes and heel, and under the arch, a space.

Dust

and

Breath

Dust and Breath
(Not a
single thing)

December 4, 1993

Butoh, Zen, and Japan have a quiet
core, like the space between thoughts,
although the surface may be tense and
ofttimes frustrated. As the Japanese
saying goes, "the nail that sticks up
will be hammered down." However
disturbing this image, it contributes
to an integrative aesthetic—although
the price of accord (might) constrain
independence, raising conflict between
community values and individuality.

One could rightly argue that defer-
ence to the group erodes individuality

and promotes a herd mentality, just as Japan has had to examine its traditional position on group loyalty since the end of World War II. The ego is perhaps no better guide than the herd, a side of the argument that flies in the face of Western individualism. The compelling self-formative ego separates from others and maybe even struggles against them for various reasons (to rebel, to excel, to state an unpopular opinion, to stand on a principle, to suppose a superiority, etc.). It rightly marks distinctions and individuates, but it also arrogates authority and plunders; the controlling ego thinks it knows what is best for everyone. Sometimes it wants out. Under duress, it longs to annihilate (through drugs and sex, for instance). When it becomes too solid, its hard core seeks the softer edges of sleep and dream. Through group support, meditation, or aesthetic submersion, the ego can also peacefully subside, not needing to assert itself. The "I" that isolates dualistically (sometimes with good reason) is not this "I."

Here we enter another perceptual strata of the self most aptly described as metaphysical. This is the Not-I of Zen, the experience of moving behind the manifest desires of the separate self. I am speaking of the Zazen (meditative) balancing of the body/mind complex through patient sitting. As the breath calms, the self becomes less self-assertive, and individuality blurs. In this way a serenity can develop where (for the time being) there is no figure (called self) and no ground (called other). Things receive equal attention because attention itself is shining (at this point); it is not compelled toward accomplishment of a specific goal. This is also evident in the practice of Zen regarding daily work, which sees all work as equal in value and draws pleasure from the doing of work *in the moment*, not the end result. Here is the peaceful "I," working without striving.

When I first started to study Zen, I attended the Zen lectures of judo master Sachio Ashida, who is also a professor of psychology at our college in Brockport, New York. (In 1998 he was recognized by the emperor of Japan for his perseverance in the true spirit of Judo, rather than selling out to popular modalities.) I once asked Ashida-sensei if the various practices of Zen aim to get rid of the ego. "No," he said, "the goal is a healthy ego, not needy, greedy, or aggressive." When judo is practiced in the Zen way it is called "gentle measure." I took his judo class and began to consciously incorporate the Zen values of body/mind centering in my dances.

Hidenori Tomozoe, a judo expert from Japan, also practices judo in the Zen way. When he came to the United States to study with my husband who teaches philosophy of sport in Brockport, this very large and obviously powerful man told me that he took a vow of nonviolence—never to use his judo skills except with a well-matched partner in a fair contest. I asked him what he would do if he were attacked. He said, "I would never use judo." So I asked him what he would do if his wife or child were being attacked, and he repeated "I would not use judo." I could hardly believe my ears, since I thought judo was a form of self-defense. He explained that judo was defensive, but only in well-matched play. His final answer to me was delivered emphatically and with a smile—"I took a vow, and there are worse things than losing your life." From the resolve in his eyes, I had to believe him. This gave me another perspective on the healthy ego (or was this a transformed ego?) that Ashida had been talking about. In the following year, I had the joy of seeing Tomo (as we call him) dance at a disco in Tsukuba, Japan. I have seen happy children dance, but never such a big one.

When I danced in a Zen Dance performance choreographed by Korean Sun Ok Lee, I learned about a Zen kind of self-inquiry in movement, one that observes and stands back from the self, not to erase the self but to be in a stream-of-action without the need for self-assertion. From Korean Zen, called *Son*, Lee cultivates a form of Zen dance that concentrates in the here and now. Her dance meditations create an atmosphere of tranquility, reverence, grace, and acceptance. As she states in her classes: "In Zen Dance, everything is accepted just as nature accepts everything." In the practice of Zen Dance, one learns how to look into the moment in which a thought or feeling enters the body. All emotions from the pleasing and joyful to those most angry are given the same notice. One does not identify with the emotion, but rather observes the source of reactions, the ground of feeling from which all emotions arise. Instead of being provoked or stimulated toward outward expressiveness, one learns how to replace habitual reactions with Zen questioning—using the Korean word "yimoko" (the quest for the true self) as a mantra for a movement meditation. This subliminal self-questioning or "answerless quest," as Lee calls it, brings about a state of nonjudgmental awareness as it moves spiritually toward a giving and self-forgiving unconditional love.

Deriving from Korean *Son*, Lee's work borrows the equivalent but more universally understood word, Zen. It partakes of an

Eastern metaphysics that equalizes time and emotional tensions; no one moment stands out. The musicality of her dance does not create a storm of tensions and resolutions, as is typical in the West's classical and romantic music, for instance. Its Zen time is present time, all time, not held back or surging forward but existing in the middle.

One can hear such centering of time values and relaxation of tensional drive in the contemporary music of Japanese composer Toru Takamitsu. He configures tones as clusters that float in space: *A Flock Descends Into the Pentagonal Garden* (1977) is a good example of his work. Similar valuings of tone and time entered into contemporary music of the West, but with a more intellectually derived aesthetic based in strict rules of distributive counterpoint. This began with the twelve-tone music of Arnold Schoenberg (1874–1951), giving equal value to every tone of the diatonic scale, deconstructing chromatic tension in the dominant-subdominant-tonic relationship. Western deconstruction of linear time finally found its way into the hypnotic, structurally repetitious music mantras of Philip Glass in the postmodern period.

In present-centered aesthetics, dissonance and consonance can be equally valued, tone given space, and space given breath. The spaces between tones in music as between breaths in the body become eloquent in present-centered aesthetics when consciousness has the opportunity to shift from its forward orientation to experience relief. Moments empty of thought and habit as we let go the compulsion to act or even think upon them. We learn the value of doing nothing, of clearing a space of its excess furniture.

Such emptiness resonates in the style of Japan's culture. It is there in the austerity of Zen and Noh theater, in the quiet minimal gestures of the tea ceremony as well as the social restraint of the Japanese—despite those noisy business deals being cut in Tokyo's restaurants nightly, the flamboyance of the Kabuki, or the maximal angularity of Issey Miyaki's fashion design. While Miyaki is bold, his lines are spacious and uncluttered, often leaving the literal shape of the body to the imagination. (In 1998, in a playful communal gesture, he designed a single dress of long, unrolling fabric to be worn by twenty-three women at once. His designs for dance and for grandmothers alike are equally imaginative.) What the Japanese leave unstated is crucial. In Japan, one learns how to look at the space surrounding a painting, and to listen to the pauses and silences in conversation and music.

Silence is at the heart of Butoh also; although its theatrical means vary greatly from one company to another. When the curtain goes up on a Sankai Juku performance and the first images materialize, my mind clears of its noise and begins to float.

Sankai Juku's Shijima (*The Darkness Calms Down in Space*) explores a beige and sandy silence. Like a Zen koan, or riddle, it promotes frustration of linear thought to release a mystical silence known as *mu* or emptiness. Strictly speaking it is not Zen, but it works aesthetically toward the same quietude, evoking a meditative pace and relaxed observation where images softly brush the mind: disturb, awaken, and flower equally and uninterruptedly for an hour and a half. It was choreographed by master stylist Ushio Amagatsu in 1988 with music by Yoichiro Yoshikawa and Yas-Kas. Some Butoh, like that of Min Tanaka, is more pedestrian in nature. Not Sankai Juku. It is highly polished theater and, like the designs of

Shijima is a work choreographed for Sankai Juku dance company by its founder Ushio Amagastu. High up the burnished wall a figure steps out in space, while dancers below create human calligraphy against the light-reflecting, pounded surface. The photograph demonstrates the architectural disposition of Sankai Juku. *Photo © Dalahaye.*

Issey Miyaki, it is maximal minimalism. No motions are wasted and there is economy of color and line, but at the same time a generous theatricality.

The dancers in *Shijima* are distillations of time, the space of the performance a washed ground for the dance, scrubbed and stressed —as though the world were rough rock prepared as a backdrop.

Shijima clears a time of dust and breath,

(of) four folded bodies
(that) lie—tied bundles
                          in a path of object stillness

(Its) Rough walls, pale gold
windows, glowing stone
and desert wind
                          mark the metaphysics of the space

Unravel (an) eerie dance
four dusty forms:
head, fingers,
                          legs and ribs

Thunder (rolls)
overhead white sudden light
a fifth figure
steps out in space,

high up the wall

              a burnished brown

So etched,
his mouth opens
a dark hole in his face

(Heads drop) another torso falls,
lets free the figure from the stone-
              stubborn hieroglyph

Sand falls,
Streams from the ceiling
into the ancient pool
              of time and dancing

Down through the light
in fine and swirling powders,
the dance imprints
              on sand, in time

The dust calms,
a distant bell sounds thinly through it
The dance becomes sensual,
              impersonal in space
leaves
doubts about reality

Fasten then release
the bodies from the bones,

in and out the sunwashed tones

How they are raised
to hang suspended,
outstretched wrists and arms

Time and light lift
the wounded birds,

God's imprint from a mold of sand.

The Hanging Body

Joan
Laage's
Performance
in
Brockport,
New
York

Unconscious Mind
(With no mind)

April 23, 1994

If individual personalities are limited
as the word individual suggests, then
we each are limited by dint of personality. However, some courageous
individuals stretch their own personalities beyond limits in the creation
of vital theater. Joan Laage invents a
remarkable individuality in Nothing
Lasts but Memory, throwing her self beyond self-given and culturally acquired
boundaries.

   As an American, she accomplishes
her own manner of characterization

American Butoh dancer and choreographer Joan Laage in her work *Nothing Lasts but Memory*. *Photograph by Rhoda Evans.*

stemming from the Japanese Butoh ways of moving and conceiving of the body—particularly "the hanging body" and "the body adorned." Her dance, *Nothing Lasts but Memory*, is a highly detailed embodiment of an anonymous old woman in a brown dress. She is covered with randomly placed white gloves and wears sturdy block-heeled black shoes that shuffle and clatter about. Indecisive adjustments of feet, unsteady posture, and faded grimacing overlay her imminent annihilation.

Within the tragic shadow of the dance, however, there is light and explosive energy. The nostalgia is not of the sweet variety; rather, it seeks memory with strength, most apparent in the many ways of handling a string of shoes bound together. Sometimes she rests on the pile and handles it tenderly. Toward the end, she swings the shoes in arcs and lets them drop from a height as she climbs a ladder. Laage has taken the thematic of shoes imagistically from shoes of the Holocaust. The entire dance is inspired by a newspaper article about a woman employed in a museum where she cleaned shoes of victims of the Holocaust, in which she discovered bits of ribbon and notes tucked in the linings. The dance speaks to the pain held in these remains.

In the beginning, Laage emerges from under a pile of dead leaves in front of a rope-linked ladder. At first just a white arm reaches upward out of the pile as though hanging from a string, then just as unexpectedly the whole figure rolls over on its side, entirely ashen and deathlike in the dry leaves, and just as light and empty. As in much of Butoh, Laage allows the picture to form fully in the stillness of her body, lying on her side with only the breath barely moving for a long time, like the answer to a question.

In the second half of the work, Laage sheds the drab body she so carefully constructed in the first part to enter a blue strip of light. Here she is transfigured white and naked, her back painted with black railroad tracks, lined with numbers and the imprint of barbed wire. There is hunger and vulnerability in her stances. She remains for some time in shivering stillness. Then she improvises a stumbling whip-wrapping of her body in red silk cords she pulls from the ceiling, lacing her white body with symbolic tracks of blood.

This is a dance from the left hand of God—cast totally from the *hara*—the instinctual center of the belly in Zen and the martial arts—the place of readiness and life that promotes flow, courage, and abandon. As Laage told me in a conversation, she learned through Butoh that she might create situations that would release her instinctual dance. Kazuo Ohno taught her to feel this as the place where life forms in the mother, and to dance from this place of origin and preconscious memories.

Laage's dance shows its American Zen face, but its detachment is cast against the pain of living. It is aware, as Laage said to me, of not being in this world. The dance wants to make up for—and to face—the world, like a child of abusive parents wants to be good enough to stop the beating. It is a wild dance, naked and elemental. The dance and its text written by David Thornbrugh and David Crandall encourage a broad interpretation of *Holocaust*. The string of empty shoes reminds us of the feet of those who walked to the gas chambers. In the tiny details of the dance, the painful foot binding of Chinese women can be imagined. The dance grows overall from such small means, then builds to a blind frenzy, seeking a metaphysical end. Zenlike, it finally lets go this attempt. There is no effective resolution. One feels history "nowing" itself. The dancer might do anything at this point—throw up, hurt herself? Yet she is dancing and does not forget this. It is the dance that saves her. When I saw Laage in November of this year, I asked her to describe her consciousness while dancing. She answered quickly and without editing:

Joan Laage in an inverted "hanging body" posture typical of the many butoh forms, both improvised and choreographed. *Photograph by Jan Cook*.

When I dance I sense my physical body existing in space and time. I sense my mental/spirit being present in my body, a physical body without limit of spatial three-dimensional boundary. As my mind/spirit is limitless, feeling eternity, my physical body is light, and being is effortless. When I dance, I am. I am present and yet I am absent. When I dance I don't know where I am or who I am but that I am. Somehow when I dance I become meaning.[1]

Zen

and

Wabi-Sabi

Taste

*Setsuko
Yamada's
Performance
in
Toronto*

Wabi-Sabi,
Plain and
Austere Beauty
(Slow breeze
and
bright moon)

October 6, 1995

Wabi-sabi is a Japanese aesthetic concept that has a metaphysical basis akin to that of Dogen Zen, a form that has its roots in medieval times and the austerity of "just sitting." I have been introduced to Dogen through the writings, calligraphy, and inspiration of my Zen teacher, Shodo Akane-sensei. I have also come to understand the *wabi-sabi* aesthetic in association with Zen as a plain and austere beauty infused with Zen spareness and transformation.

Wabi-sabi expresses a generation-extinction point of transformation that links it philosophically to Zen in general and to Dogen in particular. There is suggested here a natural process or cycle that is all-inclusive, an arising to fall away to begin again with no beginning and no end. Coming meets going; going is coming, and everything is coming from and returning to nothingness. Such is the metaphysical essence of *wabi-sabi*[1] as well as Zen. In both cases, nothingness is pregnant. For nothing would not be what it is without everything. Nothing is a backward everything, an unseen cloud that can shift, scuttle, and disperse, thinning consciousness to zero. When consciousness lands, the landing itself is something.

Wabi (elemental grace, rustic and ascetic) and *sabi* (objective, understated dignity and the delicate traces of time) infuse Zen. *Wabi* originally meant the loneliness of living with nature away from society. Because of its ephemeral character, *wabi* can be compared to dance, appearing and disappearing in present-centered time. Change, movement, and the pathos of nature (rather than permanence) is thus indicated. *Wabi* is called "quiet elegance" in Japanese-English dictionaries, but its elegance is not that of a flower in bloom. Instead, it refers to a somatic level of slowing down, moving back to points of inception. This is the place where buds are forming rather than blossoming, and the salmon color of the rose-to-be is barely visible at the tightly closed tip. *Sabi* meant "chill," "lean," or "withered"—the passing of the rose into obscurity, the flutter of dry leaves. Now Japanese-English dictionaries call *sabi*, "antique look."

About the fourteenth century, new and overlapping meanings evolved. *Wabi* and *sabi* together began to take on the meaning of "unprepossessing simplicity." This aesthetic can be traced back to the atmosphere of loneliness and minimalism in ninth and tenth century Chinese poetry and monochromatic ink painting. By the sixteenth century, *wabi-sabi* had permeated Japanese sophisticated culture.[2] It has continued as an indispensable element of Japanese aesthetics, particularly in the carefully planned, detailed ritual of the tea ceremony. Here minimal motion in handling tea utensils and serving guests with utmost care and respect is elevated to an art. In fact, the tea service is carried out in a dance of small steps and refined motions.

Wabi-sabi has its history in tea. The first *wabi-sabi* tea master was a Zen monk from Nara, Murata Shuko (1423–1502). He introduced consciously understated, locally produced utensils. About a hundred years later, the warlord Toyotomi Hideyoshe was making tea-ceremony rooms of pure gold (not a very *wabi-sabi* thing to do, more *hade* in taste: flashy, gaudy, and vain). It was his visit to a humble tea master in his service, Sen no Rikyu (1522–1591), and Rikyu's celebrated garden of morning glories, that turned the aesthetic tide. When Hideyoshe arrived, he found that all the morning glories had been uprooted.

The unhappy warrior repaired to Rikyu's thatched roof tea house of bare and weathered wood. There, in the alcove, glowed one perfect morning glory in a common clay pot. Hideyoshe hardly knew what to make of this, but it would prove his aesthetic undoing. From Rikyu's aesthetic innovation sprang the new sobriety of *wabi-sabi*. The conspicuously inconspicuous became the latest thing and continued as a theme. In the meantime, Hideyoshe's jealousy of Rikyu's growing acclaim eventually overcame him, prompting him to order Rikyu's ritual suicide at age seventy. As *wabi-sabi* became popular, it also became well crafted, and (as often in Japan) expensive.[3]

Today, the meanings of *wabi* and *sabi* are interchangeable, and they inform not only aesthetics, but also metaphysics.[4] They come together at the still point of aliveness where opposites ignite but never quite complete each other. Impermanence is accepted as a fact of nature to be cultivated in *wabi-sabi* metaphysical aesthetics and spirituality. Here beauty may be coaxed from ugliness, and all that is unnecessary drops away.

Beauty and ugliness themselves disappear as temporary dualisms, born of the oneness that is at the heart of Asian monism. A *wabi-sabi* beautiful ugliness may be thought of as spiritual unity consciousness that springs from oneness. Things can be split because there is *something* that can be split. The beautiful and the ugly come from the same source. Lao Tsu says: "everything is beautiful and everything is ugly." Two comes from one, and returns back to one. "One" itself (our consciousness of "things" as entities) can disappear and reappear. What we call "the self" is also subject to these shiftings (of consciousness).

Thus, the still point of illumination may arise through disparate, even conflicting elements. These are experientially understood in the Zen koan, where ambiguity is accepted, even celebrated, in riddles that defy rational terminus. Immersion in such *wabi-sabi*

koans as "what is *mu*?" (what is emptiness), or "what was my original face?" (even before my parents were born), can confuse the rational mind, propelling the unconscious into a state of enlightened
play.

Enlightenment means "to make lighter." Many in the West are
familiar with the koan meditation practice as a means to break
through the limits of rationality to the experience of enlightenment, or the pure play of consciousness. We are less familiar with
the rigors of "just sitting" that ground Dogen Zen. Whatever the
meditational means, however, the processes are leading along the
same path, one that has no final destination.

The process, "the path" or "the way" rather than the end point,
is emphasized. This process involves a conversion of action to
meditational nonaction, and what is called in Dogen Zen: "casting off the body and the mind." It is this precise point (of purification, regression, and self-effacement) that is often taken up in
Butoh. Yoko Ashikawa's classes develop this Butoh aspect in the
image of "walking behind yourself." Natsu Nakajima develops a
similar self-erasure in "killing the body" (metaphorically) by walking forward while moving consciousness backward into an imagined third eye. The Zen koan might also be at work in Butoh—
as murky (confused) movement becomes clear (like still waters)
and mind dust settles.[5] One can experience a mind-clearing similar
to that of the koan (the original face behind the social face)
in Kazuo Ohno's classes, moving peacefully in utero without
thinking.

"Casting off the body and the mind" is also evident in the

purifying *wabi-sabi* dance style of Setsuko Yamada. Unlike her post-Butoh contemporary, Saburo Teshigawara, Yamada makes conscious use of Butoh. Hers is a more classical dance, however, than previous Butoh. Yamada's dance is more formal than emotional, and quintessentially Japanese. It clears away emotion in the manner of meditation. It is a site for the merging of action and nonaction, where the active center of meditation meets the meditational core of action.

Yamada studied with Akira Kasai in his Tenshi-kan improvisational Butoh group where meditation and personal development were a part of the dance-making process. (I write of Kasai's recent work in the final chapter.) This background is apparent in her dances, and like Kasai, whose involvement with Butoh began with Hijikata and continues still today, her present work belongs to a new generation of Butoh or Butoh-influenced post-Butoh dance.

In *Forests, Gathering Honey of the Moon*, Yamada and her company Biwa-Kei collaborate with the natural sounds from Mineko Grimmer's audible sculpture and computer sounds by Mamoru Fujieda. The sculpture uses the sound of running water so typical of Zen gardens, as a small waterfall of melting ice trickles slowly into a pool of water set in a rectangular plain wood box. Over the pool in the upstage right corner, three irregularly cut slats overlap. Above hangs a cone-shaped block of ice within which are frozen a cluster of pebbles. As the ice melts during the performance, stones drop, striking the resonant wood, creating delicate "pinging" and "plopping" in the water. The additional sound score incorporates a stone flute and dancers' voices mixed with sprinklings of prepared sounds and simple drumming. Sparsely spaced sounds intermingle with the tones arising intermittently from the pool.

The aesthetic environment is both visual and auditory, but the intervals between seeing and hearing are blurred in the mixing of elements. The cradle of water immediately establishes the symbolism and mystical sensibility of the dance. One sees the dance through water, through the sounds of quiet rain. The gaze is not directed outward but is called inward, to what the Chinese call "the chamber of water," in meditation.[6] Serene luminosity is an inseparable part of the character of Yamada's aesthetic. It can be seen from her first solo work, *Lilac Garden* in 1977, through *The Crystal Vagina* in 1983, up to the present work premiered in March 1995 in Tokyo. Yamada's dance bears the heritage of Butoh, but it has made peace with dance traditions that Butoh rejected. It contains the harmonies of ballet, although not its upward aspirational character. The (sometimes) unstressed body balance of formal modern dance is also apparent. Several streams meet in *Forests, Gathering Honey of the Moon*, generating and extinguishing each other. Tradition and avant-garde experiment blend into one; past and present converge in a present-centered meditational dance. Its steady aesthetic and subtle power is created through Japanese breathing techniques, Asian inwardness, and centering techniques from tai chi. Yamada's aesthetic does not shock, as did the original Butoh. Rather, it understates, soothes, and heals.

Hanging and Receiving: Setsudo Yamada leans slightly to the side and hangs from her upward gaze toward the moonlight as she receives (or waits for) some special blessing or gentle rain. *Photograph by Joan Laage.*

For most of the full-length concert, the dancers are costumed in long tan billowy coats with a plain yet contemporary flair. Underneath is a cream white dress, and the shoes are pedestrian— soft black ankle boots. The dancer is not cast in mythical form, at least not at the outset. Instead we see at first a dancer/person in elegant but plain street clothes. Over time, the color orange is gradually added to the costumes, but just a sliver. It acts like a wisp of color on a beige and brown landscape painting or a few strokes cast in empty space on a monotone parchment scroll.

The movement is all around and within a liquid center. It is sparse and never settled. There is often a singular focus moving around the point of the eyes. The movement is not designed so that the eyes lead the focus, as they ordinarily must if one is to see where one is going. Rather the eyes become the focus, as the gaze moves inward with support from the movement. The time of the dance is never hurried; there is enough time; there is all the time in the world. Like Noh theater and meditational time, time here is about a fragile border between wakefulness and dream. But it is not wistful or wasted time. Psychologically, it is the time it takes for the ego to disperse into the atmosphere. In terms of Butoh, it is the time it takes for individual features to disappear, the time it takes for the sedimented body to erase itself, the time it takes for mind dust to clear.

Yamada's movement has more in common with the kinesphere of Chinese tai chi than the famous kinesphere of dance theorist Rudolph von Laban. The latter creates an aesthetic that places the body in spherical space with the feet on the ground. The possible movements of the limbs are then conceived directionally within this space. Tai chi, on the other hand, does not extend the body into spherical space. It ruminates smoothly within the sphere, transferring gently from one foot to another, balancing incrementally through imagistic patterns of yin/yang complements with steady flow and even containment.

Butoh often moves with just such tai chi sensitivity to surrounding space. In its rootedness, Butoh also projects the sphere below the earth, lowering the body's center of gravity. It achieves this through bending the knees and dropping the weight of the pelvis downward. This tai chi effect of Butoh is one of slow motion spherical suspension with a lowered center. Both Butoh and tai chi can thus produce a sinking feeling. Additionally, within the effortless ease of the movement, there is a floating visage, image, or sensation. The body sinks while it floats; herein lies the floating-sinking composure of Yamada's aesthetic. She dances like soft wood, half in and out of water. In fact, the warmness of wood is apparent in the colors and whorls of the dance, its sounds and motions like wood shavings: slipping, falling, piling.

Forests, Gathering Honey of the Moon seems set in a shady place, where solos open to the four cardinal corners of the earth. There is also a single pure calligraphy created in the process, one that is never ceasing, of presentness quite incomplete, gentle and cool. While the environment and movement of the dance evoke the forest, they also reveal the Japanese appreciation for nature as it becomes distilled and cultivated in miniature. This is not nature in full bloom or wildish forms. It is minimal and careful, like Zen rock gardens and manicured trees. It touches the senses lightly, precisely. In the same way, Yamada's dance evokes the subtleties of the forest (its spreading mosses and delicate ferns) and a luminous coalescence (gathering honey of the moon).

Neither is nature existing for itself in this dance. Yamada complicates it with human intervention. Her dance develops this in a post-Butoh matter-of-fact way that it introduces at the beginning. It commences with the entrance of a male dancer dressed in earth-toned chinos and a loose shirt (more *jimi* than *wabi*—just plain and casual). He walks through the audience to sit on the lower right-hand edge of the stage, and reads silently from a book. He remains there as a background (perhaps suggesting the underlying text for the dance) as Yamada enters in the softly draped coat. At first, she explores center stage, building energy gradually from a tai chi basis. The coat floats over the movement, muting it. She overlays this movement background with iconoclastic gestures in a free-form kinship with modern dance.

At some point during this progression, the reader falls over into a deep sleep, and four other dancers dressed like Yamada join her. They probe the space in pointillist fashion, not indicating a strong group center. Rather, each dancer's personal center of gravity allows the perceiver to fill in a common center or linkage. The actual center of the stage is empty. Likewise, dancers are not magnetized or pulled into each other's orbit. Neither is the audience pulled into a distinct center of focus, as in the ballet. There is nevertheless an agreeableness that evokes ballet harmonies with no intentional discord. This distinguishes Yamada's work from the expressive and tensional abrasiveness of much earlier Butoh. She employs her study of ballet in its formal objectivity while bypassing its aspirational grandeur.

The dance continues without building tension, as the dancers bring a large, flat, Victorian hat filled with feathers on stage. One by one they throw the feathers into the air. Their gentle falling might represent a clearing of the mind (of habitual thought patterns), since the dancers become interested in the unpredictability of the falling feathers as they land helter-skelter. The reader wakes up to watch the stage action from his seated position.

The energy of the dance eventually builds a greater intensity, but its time is liquid and undifferentiated. Time, I mean, is not cut into rhythmic repeatable structure in this dance. It slips from duration to duration in a non-beat sense of whole time. Presently, Yamada throws her shoes at the other dancers, a pedestrian move, not motivated by anger or play. The others then chase and catch Yamada as she falls to the floor. The chase is not vested with intention; its outcome seems unimportant, removed and abstract. The dancers pursue Yamada like random thoughts chasing an idea.

The reader gets up and leaves as unobtrusively as he appeared. This could almost be missed. He reflects the objectivity of the dance, its "distance"; or perhaps "detachment" would be a better word. As coinciding with and subliminally witnessing the dance, he is both inside and outside of its actional substance. The company of dancers also exit, one by one, to leave Yamada as she lies quietly on the floor. A column of sand falls from the ceiling to catch the light and spread out beside her. This dropping of sand in Butoh, as initiated by the Sankai Juku company, always elicits images of time and malleability. The shifting/dispersing qualities of sand in its fineness produces an aesthetic tendency toward disappearance—like that of impermanent Tibetan sand paintings in intricate forms of mandalas or erosions around rocks washed by the sea.

The lighting changes in this section to cast a reflection of ripples from the water sculpture onto the backdrop. The water and background are stirred by the occasional dropping of pebbles. Presently Yamada also stirs. Becoming more alive to an objective world, she focuses her vision to see things around her. She walks upstage and removes the wood slats from the pool of water. She dips her arm in the pool to further awaken to the ambience of the environment. Then she dances alone, attendant to time and its passing. The others gradually join her to end the dance with a unison gesture, the only one in the dance. They all fall on their sides, forming a semi-circle on the floor. Each dancer faces the audience from her vantage point in the circle of bodies. This unity of movement and focus is not a completion, however. The dance remains wispy, ready to dissemble and begin again as the lights fade.

The dance contains dynamic stillness, like candles mirrored in water or mind-shiftings at dusk. Aglow with unprotected presence, the body is attuned to the space below, its grounding dance loosened as a lowering of muscle tension provokes keener hearing. A pebble has the last word in this nondecorative but elegant dance. *Forests, Gathering Honey of the Moon* leaves a magical afterimage of *wabi-sabi* shiftings between Yamada and the group (self and others)—rarified, well crafted, spiritual.

The *wabi-sabi* of Yamada's dance is commensurate with the Japanese aesthetics of imperfection and insufficiency that Yuriko Saito writes about in its relationship to Zen. One of the bounds to be overcome in Zen enlightenment is our natural tendency to appreciate the perfect, the opulent, and the gorgeous while being disappointed and dissatisfied with the opposite qualities. They are equally valuable for manifesting their own Buddha nature.[7]

As an aspect of imperfection, Zen introduces the kind of transience that I find in Yamada's dance: "If man were never to fade away like the dews of Adashino, never to vanish like the smoke over Toribeyama, but lingered on forever in the world, how things would lose their power to move us! The most precious thing in life is its uncertainty."[8]

The

Community

Body

Akira
Kasai
and
Yumiko
Yoshioka
in
San
Francisco

Unidentified
(Left open
to the
imagination)

August 24th, 1997

"Butoh Festival"—isn't that an oxy-moron? Perhaps, but San Francisco hosts a successful annual Butoh Festival through the Dancers' Group organiza-tion serving the Bay Area where Butoh is celebrated as a popular dance move-ment. The festival draws appreciative audiences, and Butoh classes fill up and close out before the festival. How does one celebrate the dance of darkness or "the dead body" that sustains it? Akira Kasai shows us how as he carries what

Portrait of Akira Kasai by Kevin Bubriski.

he terms "the community body" with him through his festival performances and classes.

To write closely about his performance of the dead body, I should drop my own body, my conscious body, and just improvise —abandon and throw my heart, tear apart the clouds. But exposition intervenes, and thought waves form otherwise.

Two untrained dancers—or half-trained—performed against Kasai's solo dance at the festival, *Are We Carrying Our Bodies into the World of the Dead?* Sho Terasaki and Mitsu Kasai (Akira's son) framed him like dead bookends. They distracted me; but over time, I began to lose them. Kasai's dancing consumed the stage—so unaware of its effect, it might have been a dead man dancing. As in my interview with him, which follows below, Kasai's dance exposes the central Butoh concept of killing the material body.

Kasai's method of performance is improvisation of the sort that obviates the body. For more than thirty years, he has been inventing and reinventing his improvisational approaches, as one of the first to perform with Butoh founders Tatsumi Hijikata and Kazuo Ohno in the 1960s. Kasai set up Tenshi-Kan (The House of the Angels) as a school and performing group in 1970. In 1979 he moved to Germany to study eurythmy, a dancelike form of body training founded by German mystic philosopher Rudolf Steiner (1861–1925) in 1912. Kasai began performing Butoh again in 1994 with *Seraphita*. Since then he has been performing internationally with a full-spectrum Butoh, not necessarily dark and slow, but of many colors and bright speeds.

It would not be right to associate him entirely with new Butoh styles, however. Kasai is the most obvious continuing bridge to the original Butoh. And in my conversations with him at the festival, I came to understand that he eschews the emphasis placed on originality in the West, a sentiment also expressed by the other featured performer in the festival, Yumiko Yoshioka. As I have experienced in Japan, the teacher and the primogeniture is honored, even in an antitraditional form like Butoh. The self is secondary, and novelty is not appreciated for its own sake. Butoh can renew and change, but new is not necessarily better. Connections to others and the past are more important than individualism.

Kasai dates back to the original impulse of Butoh as based on the physically imperfect body of people from the northeastern part of Japan where Hijikata came from. The stooped and clumsy postures of old people and bodies deformed by difficult conditions through long periods of time became the model for Butoh, but its goal was nonrepresentational. Hijikata's Butoh sought (almost mystically) to embody (to become) the object imaged. The materiality of the body is transformed in Butoh. Referential movement is not the goal as in Western mimesis, symbolism, or exemplification. Neither is movement-in-itself the goal as in much modern/postmodern dance. From Hijikata's dance forward, Butoh dissipates Western material form and aesthetic mirroring.

Like Hijikata, Kasai peels away his body's armor, but for a wider purpose. Kasai has planetary concerns that go beyond Hijikata's theater of the Japanese body: Kasai seeks to develop the community body.

Interview with Akira Kasai
(Translation by Mikio Hirata)

August 22, 1997

Fraleigh: Mr. Kasai, you were one of the first to dance with Hijikata and Ohno as Butoh developed. You danced with them in *Rosy Dance* in 1965. I thought the part of this dance you showed on film here at the festival was quite whimsical and showed a lighter side of Butoh. What do you remember about Hijikata?

Kasai: He developed something totally new which is conceptually based. If you compare Butoh to German expressionism, Ohno is a more obvious link than Hijikata.

Fraleigh: And Hijikata? What is he close to?

Kasai: Rather than connecting to any other dance, he connected to painting and to literature. This does not mean that he was interested in dance narrative, however. It was the literature of the twentieth century that influenced Hijikata, and surrealism in art.

Fraleigh: Did Hijikata relate to "theater of the absurd" then?

Kasai: I have often spoken with Hijikata about Beckett. We discussed Samuel Beckett's *Waiting for Godot.* He thought very highly of this work. Hijikata congealed the esoteric absurd in dance movement. The tendency for him while developing his work was to get away from the constraints of time—spacing the time element, or changing the timing to space, turning the story into object art rather than abstracting it. Symbolism was totally opposite from his style. For instance, the cross is a Christian symbol that embodies a time period and a story. Hijikata did not work with such literal symbolism.

Fraleigh: How about your own work and symbolism?

Kasai: I studied with Ohno and learned symbolic expression from him. I also learned Hijikata's mode of depiction. Spontaneous improvisation furthered Hijikata's way of objectifying everything. So I carry both ways in my own work.

Ohno's work *Old Man and the Sea* is highly symbolic. At the end, the fisherman is drawing a dead fish out of the water. Ohno did this work before meeting Hijikata. After meeting Hijikata, his strong symbolism crumbled somewhat.

Fraleigh: When did you study with Hijikata and Ohno?

Kasai: I studied with Ohno from 1961–63 and with Hijikata from 1964–66. I worked on stage with Hijikata. My first solo concert was in 1966. Those six years' time working with Ohno and Hijikata were very formative for me. Ohno makes you work with the power of the imagination, and with Hijikata you objectify everything. I need them both.

Fraleigh: Now it seems that your work clears a path from the contemporary Butoh back to the original but nevertheless offers something new. I know it is difficult to look at oneself, but what do you feel is your uniqueness in Butoh?

Kasai: I work with dance as it involves the changing of the senses. If your senses do not change, the dance does not change. The consciousness of the body comes into the picture with the changing of the senses. Generally we believe that in dance no matter what happens in our senses the physicality does not change. But to me, when the senses change, consciousness changes, and the physical body itself changes. In a bigger sense is the larger question: "What is matter?" So with sense and consciousness working together, the physical body itself does change, matter changes. Still further is *maya*. In a very Eastern way matter is *maya*.

Fraleigh: Do you mean *maya* in the Hindu sense—*maya* as illusion or the veil of this existence?

Kasai: Yes. When you get down to this level you should be able to see what the physical body really is. Dance eliminates the physical self.

Fraleigh: I think the concepts that you are speaking about have

Akira Kasai improvising. *Photograph © Kevin Bubriski.*

roots in Buddhism and Hinduism. Do you ever think about these roots in religion?

Kasai: The understanding of matter between East and West is entirely different. In the West, matter is body. In the East, there is ultimately no matter. Dancing spans from the body of matter to the nonmaterial larger body.

Fraleigh: Do you think of these things when you are choreographing?

Kasai: These *are* the concepts of my choreography. Choreography is not the process of shaping matter but of creating content. Without concepts you cannot choreograph. In order to teach dancers the movement, you are giving them concepts.

Fraleigh: I find this conceptual approach similar to my studies with Mary Wigman in Germany. In fact, my first Butoh classes rang true to my experience with German expressionism, but the guiding concepts were not the same.

Kasai: Butoh conceives of the body as a corpse—a dead body.

Fraleigh: In Soto Zen, they say "body and mind *is* falling off," falling away. [Body and mind are combined in the nondualistic singular verb.] Is this similar to the dead body of Butoh?

Kasai: Perhaps. You can see the body better when it is in the state of a corpse. This is Butoh.

Fraleigh: Is the corpse walking and nevertheless alive?

Kasai: The best walking is a death row inmate being led to his death.

Fraleigh: Why?

Kasai: He is stepping toward certain death. So in his steps the power of death is alive. This is definitely not like walking to a picnic. In going to a picnic, you won't see any walking really. But on death row, you can see the walking—very moving walking.

Fraleigh: This reminds me of the American movie with Susan Sarandon, *Dead Man Walking*. Maybe it is a Butoh movie.

Kasai: I see you laugh [he smiles], but "Butoh" is not really a genre. *It defines total presence.* Vaslav Nijinski and Isadora Duncan were both Butoh in my opinion, and Mary Wigman's *Witch Dance* is Butoh. After all, "bu" just means "dance," and "to" means "step." Ankoku Butoh is "a dance of darkness."

Wigman embodies European mysticism. She was influenced by Rudolph Laban who was of course a Mason. She had connections with esoteric sources. What is important in Wigman's ideas is that she does not necessarily believe in matter, but rather her work is about the soul. And the soul is living or screaming in the physical self.

Fraleigh: Wigman's witch was wild and untamed, so perhaps Hijikata can be compared with her. Laban was not so outrageous.

Kasai: Laban was more theoretical.

Fraleigh: Let me ask you about the first workshop I took from you, and "the community body" that you talked about. Is this important in your dancing?

Kasai: This is the most important. The fingernail does not grow apart from the body, and the body of a human being does not grow apart from the community. It grows with the community, and that community includes all things in nature, not just the human community. No matter how hard dancers train—even if they are in superb condition—if they are not concerned for the larger body of nature, the dancer's body they develop does not mean much. This is one of the new concepts in dance. Your body does not develop unless you develop the community as well.

Fraleigh: This is an important idea in terms of our position in history, our ecological body.

Kasai: The human body and the earth are deeply connected. No matter how well-developed the human body may be, if we ignore the planet we do not develop. So far we say the human being has been granted power through the earth, and now the reverse is happening. Now we can revive the earth. We can! So far we have taken power from the earth; now it is time to return it. The earth is losing power; now humankind has to give it back. This is an important new Butoh concept.

Fraleigh: Was this concept there with Hijikata and Ohno?

Kasai: No. But they laid a framework. In dance from this point on we have to connect planetary elements and humankind. The reason I am able to get to this concept is because I was trained by Ohno and Hijikata.

Fraleigh: I have recognized in Butoh a great respect for nature, even though Butoh is highly theatrical. I have also seen that the love of nature in Japan is being washed away through modern commercial influences.

Kasai: There are nature elements in Butoh. But the dance is not an ecological movement or a political movement. It is a movement toward healing, just as certain words and movements can heal. It was the same in ancient times. Words were given that could heal. When words lost power, medicine came into being. Through dance we reach down into the earth. Moving into the twenty-first century I see that dance will divide into two streams—one more technical and mechanical, and the other one connecting intuitively to the earth.

Fraleigh: Perhaps we see this happening already. Butoh seems to have gone another direction than highly codified technical dance.

One last question: What is the place of the ego in Butoh?

Kasai: To discard it. But without having the ego you can't discard it.

Fraleigh: What is the ego?

Kasai: The center of the universe.

Fraleigh: Do we find and discard this center in dancing?

Kasai: In dancing, we carry our body away from ourselves.

Festival Performance, Continued

Kasai performed the same dance on the four evenings of the San Francisco Butoh festival from August 21–24. Those who saw all of the performances said they differed radically. I didn't see the first one, but heard that it was awful. This is certainly a possibility even for seasoned performers like Kasai, and improvisation opens a wide window for failure. It risks everything, and in this sense Kasai is a high flyer without a net. From his fourth performance at the festival, I return to my impressions:

He begins with a pelvis-jutting Elvis Presley pose, then evolves through constantly changing styles and figures. Embodying (becoming) the other, Kasai recalls Nijinski's two-dimensional archaic poses at one point and Isadora Duncan's dramatic range and romantic form at others. Like Duncan, Kasai can be powerful, soul-searching, and innocent, but the effect overall is chaotic. Like

Nijinski, Kasai gets lost in the dance and follows it wherever it takes him.

A light lyrical jazz ensues from the pelvic thrust. Everything melts into oscillating curves and syncopated rhythmic changes. The music of Ryoichi Sakamoto increases the flowing flavor. As the improvisation heats up with images succeeding each other at a hectic pace, I gradually become aware that Kasai is "letting go" as we typically say, or letting go of his body—"killing his body" —as Butoh would say. He is simply dancing for us, letting go of concepts altogether. The excitement is in not knowing where the next movement or shape will come from as it issues out of the blue and through the body-of-dance that Kasai has been culti- vating through his training in Butoh and other movement forms. Steiner's eurythmy slips by, included but unnoticed, as Kasai's performance gives human kinetic form to sound and sense.

Kasai's moments of lightness shift through balletic modes at times. It is odd to see Butoh faces—shock, pain, laughter, glee, howling, and squirming—suddenly burst out of balletic move- ment. Kasai skims the stage surface with a speed and physicality not typical in Butoh. An edgy jazz violin grates against his now- and-then softness. Sometimes Kasai pierces his own flow with fiery jabs and falls. A sudden leap staggers back after the landing and crumples to the floor with one leg bearing the entire descent. It reverses immediately, rerunning the movement backward from the one-legged squat landing.

| | |

Put one leg on top of the other—
and you'll understand the origin of legs.
You are merely maintaining your posture—
as you gaze in envy at bodies in movement.

Tatsumi Hijikata

Kasai is fifty-six years old and amazingly wiry and strong. His body is small and finely tuned to the atmosphere. He can pounce and undulate like a cat. In fact his demeanor on the whole is very feline, as alert stretches coincide with implacable stillness. He becomes possessed by the momentum of his dance, perfecting tart faces and nose-sniffing whole body shimmers. Sometimes he phrases with poking gestures, eyes turned askance. His mouth curls sideways and his eyes sometimes roll as his dance becomes progressively more rubbery, sweaty, and connected through the spine. He is thrown away and detached from results. As the moment carries itself, he gathers and rides its wave—less matter than light and speed. The dance turns to ominous shaking, explosions with nonstop timing. At the end, he slips away from the action, leaving it to envy. The residual energy vibrates the empty space.

Did he carry his body into the world of the dead? His program notes address the audience: "You who are face to face with my dance now! I never doubted your existence, even a moment. . . ."

| | |

This is more dance-dance than theater-dance with minimal costumes and no special lighting effects or set. Kasai wears draped dark jersey pants with a black net shirt and moves adroitly in soft jazz boots. He might be casually dressed for a Tokyo night spot. There is one change of costumes into blue and lime-green dance pants with a T-shirt. There are no ideas to follow, just the amazing amount and concentration of his jump into dance. He gives generously and wildly like Hijikata, and his face reflects a rainbow of emotions and gestures like Ohno.

August 23, 1997

Yumiko Yoshioka shared the festival performances with Kasai. In her lengthy solo work *It's All Moonshine*, Yoshioka's bare back is turned to the audience for nearly one-third of the time. For a long time, the light grows on her figure as she sits in the stillness. After a while, her shoulder blades pinch together and lift like wings.

The careful illumination gels a visual form. Her back dimples and dents from the movement and shadows. I thought I saw owl eyes. Through time, the parts and pieces of her back take on features of shadow puppetry. Her hands extending out from opposing sides of front folded arms (as seen from the back) show only palms and fingers. They become small wings perched on her shoulders before she dissolves this opening episode and moves gradually toward a pyramid of sand in the corner of the stage.

It is not actually clear what the shape is made of until she buries her head in it. At this point the dance becomes more kinetic and less visual. Yumiko eats the sand and spits it out, making insect

Yumiko Yoshioka in her opening sitting dance performs with her back to the audience in *It's All Moonshine*. Photograph © *Kazunori Ishizuka*.

gritty sounds through her teeth, then tosses the sand high in the air. She dips her long hair in the sand over and over, flipping it around, spraying the space. As she becomes crusted with the sand, she invokes a beige neutrality and curious mummification ritual, recalling the Butoh of Sankai Juku.

Space and form flow into time. Yumiko curls into the yoga child's pose, kneeling with her head on her knees facing the audience on a diagonal. From here she lifts her dress exposing the roundness of her bare buttocks, her beige garment wadded around her middle. When she stands, it falls into a skirt leaving her torso bare. She faces the audience with her sand-covered chest commencing a pogo stick jumping mixed with gyrating, spinning-spitting, and snaking movement. The dance culminates in a lizardlike licking of the space in the direction of the moon. Yoshioka's neck stretches out with her tongue as she laps, licks, and shakes through the ending.

| ₁ |

Yoshioka's work is based in Germany where she choreographs and performs with the German-Japanese Butoh dance theater group tatoeba-Theatre Danse Grotesque. She is also a longtime member of the first Japanese women's Butoh dance group, Ariadone, a company that turned away from the masculinist authority in Butoh. For twenty-five years she has performed in Japan and throughout Europe, but this performance at the San Francisco Butoh Festival 1997 marks her first performance in America. She is now a resident and member of Broellin Castle—an interna-

Yumiko Yoshioka demonstrates the disposition of Butoh toward visual art and meditative architectures. "I hope my friends will crush my bones and eat them when I'm gone, so that I may dance forever," says Yoshioka. *Photograph © Michael Peters.*

tional theater research location for multimedia art just outside Berlin. A German Butoh dancer, Delta Ra'i, who founded tatoeba-Theatre Danse Grotesque in Berlin in 1987, directed the festival performance as stage and art designer for Yoshioka.

| | |

Two days before her festival performance I took a dance class with Yoshioka, and we had time to talk over shushi after class at *We Be Shushi* in the Mission district of San Francisco. It was the best shushi (for the price) and informal Butoh interview I could have hoped for. Yoshioka talked a great deal about her consciousness as a Butoh dancer. Yes, *consciousness* was the word she used over and over:

> When I dance, sometimes I really forget what I am and where I am. I seem in between elements. So I cannot forget myself completely, but I am in between consciousness and unconsciousness. I am body, and I am soul, in between this world and another. When I dance I am a medium. There is a tension between the audience and my "self" that creates this circulation. My performance activates energy and the audience gives back the energy. There is a spiral of energy if the performance is good.

When she spoke of herself as a catalyst and bridge for the audience, I was reminded of how shamanic healing works through dance—in dance that catalyzes and changes the body, that is, like trance dance. Butoh touches this place in the body—the depth of dreams in cellular memory and our evolutionary kinship with other creatures: frogs and dolphins, insects and reptiles, birds and whales. Yoshioka's Butoh is familiar with the darkness of caves, the aliveness of the sea and the forest, our dwelling in the poetics of time.

She spoke of God as a principle of nature, a view I have often encountered in Zen, and at the heart of Shinto—the ancient religion of Japan with its female priestesses. Yoshioka further outlined her choreographic process from this principle: "When I start working, I am a catalyzer. I give birth, and the piece starts growing. I just give it an impulse, and it grows. The dance changes as everything is changing. As its unchanging principle, it connects."

Inevitably the conversation turned to Hijikata. Yoshioka told me that Hijikata's recognition of life as an improvisation had inspired her. "If Hijikata were alive today, his dance would still be changing," she said. He grew up in Tohoku in the country and wanted to create a *Tohoku Kabuki*, to reach another level of "people's theater" (Kabuki originated as a popular theater of the people). If he were alive, he would look more toward human commonalties and out toward the global body, not just the Japanese body. Hijikata said, "Northeast exists everywhere in the world." Northeast is outside the center, and this outside can be found everywhere. This is the forgotten world, the real Butoh. The word *Butoh* may only exist in the museum.

"Yes," I said to Yoshioka as I remembered my home in upstate New York, "Northeast is everywhere."

September 13, 1997

The adults must seem an ecstatic mystery to the baby's eyes,
eyes that float in a dish of tears.

Tatsumi Hijikata

Now I consider how every direction is possible in dance, "moving as all eyes," as an American dancer in Kasai's class expressed
his experience of Butoh. "I had so many eyes it was hard to know
what I was seeing," he said. "I just tried to see everything."

In his Butoh classes, Kasai creates improvisational structures
to enlarge the body beyond personal boundaries. He teaches that
we dance to develop the community body, and that the real body
is not what you see. My notes from his September 13 class help
me to better grasp this concept, especially the quotations I gathered from his descriptions in motivating dancers' improvisations:

There are many ways of living. They are all our body. There is
a deep connection with the outside and our physical selves as
we develop the outside world. We develop the community
body as we develop our physical body in dance. The sensations
of your body must also reach out.

There is an axis running through your body. You are turning
on this axis always. Your body is the rotation.

Stamping, you become light with speed, as the snowflakes
fall and lightning flashes in the sky. The floor is solid under
you. Your dance has no beginning. It has already begun, and
there is no ending. There was never a big bang before. The big
bang is now, and we are building a community body.

Breathe in and imagine this light.

We do not push against gravity, we float up. If there were only gravity, we could not stand up. There is a floating energy also.

When something cuts the floating power, we fall down.

As you breathe in, bring your hands above your head and allow yourself to float up. As you breathe out, cut the power of the floating and come down. Feel the power of gravity.

Not merely moving, accompany your movements with the awareness of physical sensation. Feel blue as you go up, for instance, or yellow as you come down.

When was I born, and when will I die? Was I here before I was born? Has my physical being always existed?

Still feel the lifting force as you go down. It takes a lot of concentration to feel up when you go down. Ask yourself: What does this floating have to do with my birth and death? Go up with the feeling of the force of gravity. Will there be gravity after my death? Did I float before my birth?

In a zero gravity field, the dancer creates gravity and floating. Imagine zero gravity and let your breath do the rest.

Is there no earth? Did the planet dissolve? Does this floating come from within ourselves?

I danced in the class despite my back pain, and sat out only long enough to gather some of Kasai's words on paper. For a long time we dancers played in a zero-gravity field creating our bodies of floating and gravitational powers. Toward the end of the class, I noticed my own body in touch with the other dancers, and I think I understood something (for the moment) about our common body. I was not conscious of making shapes or of creating rhythms, nor did I ask myself how I might have looked or seemed to an outside eye. My breath was calm and peaceful, and my pain had spread wide to a vanishing point. Humiliation is so close to humility, I thought, as I separated from the others and the Butoh therapeutic of body contact.[1] I sat alone briefly with my Zen koan at the end of class, and still no answers. "What was my face before my parents were born?"

| | |

A baby rubbing its face
is in fact peeling off the dried scum of its tears.
The wisdom to exchange a scab for a caramel
may have its origin here.
Ecstasy comes to the child
when the dried surface cracks.

Tatsumi Hijikata (translated by Kazue Kobata and Arturo Silva)

Notes

Introduction

1. Camille Hardy, "Kazuo Ohno." Review, *Dance Magazine* 70, no. 5 (May 1996): 81–82.

2. *Asian* might eventually come to mean "most of the world," Kathleen Frazer speculates as she observes the broad inclusiveness of the Third Annual Asian Festival in Toronto. See Frazer's book review of *Looking Out: Perspectives On Dance and Criticism in a Multicultural Word*, ed. David Gere with Lewis Segal et al. (New York: Schirmer Books, 1995), in *Dance Research Journal* 29, no. 1 (spring 1997): 75–78. Much of North American culture (especially its dance) might already be "African," to look in another direction and acknowledge the influence of Africa. In "Stripping the Emperor," Brenda Dixon Gottschild argues that an African aesthetic underlies the choreography of George Balanchine and propels the dance and culture of North America. See Dixon Gottschild's article in *Looking Out*. We also note that Hispanics as the fastest-growing ethnic group in America represent a sweeping fusion of race, culture, and aesthetics. Cross-cultural fusions are moving ever closer to our core.

3. Susan Blakeley Klein, *Ankoku Buto: The Premodern and Postmodern Influences on the Dance of Utter Darkness* (Ithaca: East Asia Series, Cornell University Press, 1988), 37.

4. J. Hiller, *Japanese Color Prints* (London: Phaidon Press Ltd., 1991), 6.

5. Parody, travesty, burlesque, and analogue as aspects of *Ukiyo-e* are explored by Hiller, 23.

6. Donald Richie, *A Lateral View: Essays on Contemporary Japan*, rev. ed. (Tokyo: Japan Times, Ltd., 1991), 133.

7. Sondra Fraleigh, "Chiyoe Matsumoto: Mother of Dance Education in Japan," *Dance Teacher Now* (Oct. 1996): 88–95.

8. Eastern thought began to enter into Western philosophy through Schopenhauer, then through Nietzsche at the foundation of existentialism. Schopenhauer was influential in Nietzsche's thought.

9. "The bug-ambulation" is described in detail by Kayo Mikami in her book *The Body as Vessel: Tatsumi Hijikata—An Approach to the Techniques of Ankoku-Butoh* (Tokyo: ANZ-Do Publications, 1993). I experienced the bug-ambulation and other images described here in workshops of Ashikawa and Nakajima, further described in later chapters. In a workshop with Yukio Waguri in Tokyo in October 1992, I experienced still other Butoh-inspired improvisatory stimulus: swallowing a lightning bolt, disappearing in bee pollen, developing the movements of a chicken with special attention to the eyes, neck, and facial focus in relation to the feet, and standing in a yoga lotus position on one leg forever.

10. Jean Viala and Nourit Masson-Sekine, *Butoh: Shades of Darkness* (Tokyo: Shufunotomo Co. Ltd., 1988), 16.

11. Exhibitions held in Amsterdam between 1989 and 1990 show the recent tendency to link Butoh and German expressionism, as pointed out by researcher Kazuko Kuniyoshi in her paper, "Current Trends in Butoh Research," at the Japan Asia Dance Event '93 (August 1993), Tokyo.

12. This is stated in the "Biography of Kazuo Ohno," his six-page vita.

13. Mary-Jean Cowell with Satoru Shimazaki, "East and West in the Work of Michio Ito," *Dance Research Journal* 26, no. 2 (fall 1994): 11–22, 11.

14. Ibid., 19–20.

15. Torii Kiyotada's color woodcut *Ukiyo-e* (1710–1740) shows an actor of the Ichikawa clan, probably the second Danjuro, in a dance movement of violent motion that is particularly chaotic, angular, and fierce in expression. Hijikata's chaotic Butoh pastiche develops similar qualities at the root of Butoh. Danjuro is surrounded with a swirling and starkly squared

costume in a fit of motion. (The Metropolitan Museum of Art [New York], Harris Brisbane Fund, 1949, no. 3075.)

16. Many years after leaving the school in 1977, I choreographed a *Dreh Monotonie* (turning monotony) from my remembrance of Wigman. She had described her original *Dreh Monotonie*, and I had seen Dore Hoyer's dance on this theme. My dance was an interpretation of this thematic from the expressionist period and not a reconstruction. First it established a circling in place with repetitive arm gestures to the accompaniment of a single Chinese gong. I did the same phrase over and over to the point of dizziness until I became proprioceptively accustomed to the exertion. This I conceived as a circular meditation, a ritual return and repetition—or life line. The center part of the dance accompanied by percussion was a straight/interrupted line of existential finitude, exploring the unrestrained and maddening witch. Blackouts separated the parts, so they seemed like separate dances. The third part took up the first, as though the second had never happened, and accelerated the whirling into the final fade.

17. See Joan Laage on German expressionism as a major root of Butoh in "Embodying the Spirit: The Significance of the Body in the Contemporary Japanese Dance Movement of Butoh" (Ph.D. dissertation, Programs in Dance, Texas Woman's University, Denton, Texas, August 1993), 6–8.

18. Ohno's six-page vita/biography states that he studied with Baku Ishii in 1933. Ishii as we noted had studied the new German dance with Kosaku Yamada. The biography notes that Ohno's experience of seeing expressionist Harald Kreutzberg (a student of Mary Wigman) dance in 1934 influenced him to study with Takaya Eguchi and Souko Miya in 1936. Eguchi and Miya had studied with Wigman and returned to Japan to teach the new German dance.

19. Aesthetic exchange between Japan and the West developed from world trade and travel after Japan opened its doors to foreigners in 1868. By the late nineteenth century and in the early twentieth century, Japanese woodcut prints had become wildly fashionable in Europe and the United States—scholars and collectors became connoisseurs. The French impres-

sionists Edouard Manet, Edgar Degas, Henri de Toulouse-Lautrec, and Paul Gauguin, and American Mary Cassatt shared an admiration of the Ukiyo-e woodcuts. See, especially, Colta Feller Ives, *The Great Wave: The Influence of Japanese Woodcuts on French Prints* (New York: Metropolitan Museum of Art, 1974).

20. Graham can be observed dressing her hair in the upswept ornamented style of Ukiyo-e for Jocasta in the film *A Dancer's World*. She resembles especially Utamaro's *Portrait of the Oiran Hinzauru* (color woodcut, about 1796, Art Institute of Chicago). For a fuller discussion of the global influences of Ukiyo-e on modern dance and the specific influence of Michio Ito in the cultural exchanges of modern dance, see Jonette Lancos, "Global Influences, Ukiyo-e" and "Michio Ito" in "The Movement Style and Technique of Charles Weidman" (master's thesis, Department of Dance, State University of New York College at Brockport, September 1991).

21. During the first decade of the twentieth century, dance in the United States often consisted of trite Oriental imitations in the forms of ballet, interpretive dance, and Delsarte-Orientalism. The dance world seemed intoxicated with the exotic and Oriental, even the Ballets Russes. In 1910 Fokine created the exotic ballets *Scheherazade, Cleopatra,* and *L'Oiseau de Feu.* In 1906, Ruth St. Denis created *Radha,* based on a Hindu legend, and in 1913 she premiered *O-Mika,* a Japanese dance drama. In 1928, Charles Weidman created *Japanese Actor* and *Singhalese Drum Dance* inspired by his work with artists Mei-lan Fan and Koshiro Matsumoto on Denishawn's Oriental Tour of 1925–26. Ted Shawn choreographed *The Cosmic Dance of Siva* in 1926.

22. Ernst Scheyer, "The Shapes of Space: The Art of Mary Wigman and Oskar Schlemmer," in *Dance Perspectives* 41 (New York: Dance Perspectives Foundation, 1970), 20. Scheyer writes that in Dresden in the middle twenties, Wigman's interest in the East was reinforced by her contacts with the Dresden Ethnological Museum and with Felix Tikotin who exhibited his full collection of Oriental art in the Gallery Arnold in 1923. Victor Magito, a mask carver who had experimented with Japanese Noh

masks, was also in Dresden where his wife studied at the Wigman School. Magito created the mask for *Ceremonial Figure,* 1925.

23. Scheyer, 23.

24. Modern dance incorporated the then Far East as "Oriental" and also borrowed from the South Sea Islands and Africa in its fascination for undulating rhythms, bold shapes, and abstract masks that it deemed "primitive." Louis Horst taught modern dance composition as "a sophisticated form of primitivism," as I experienced in his modern forms class. The artifacts and rituals of Native America also inspired the emerging modern dance (through Martha Graham, Eric Hawkins, and Ted Shawn), as did black music in the United States, Negro spirituals, and jazz. Eventually, black artists themselves effected the African diaspora in modern dance. Katherine Dunham was the first important modern dance pioneer fusing modern dance and black culture through African sources.

25. Jennifer Dunning, "Death-Life Celebration by *Muteki-Sha* Troupe," *New York Times,* Sunday, October 29, 1989.

26. "Numerous examples of what could be called 'rituals of inversion' can be drawn from folk rituals: the grotesque dance of the twisted-faced Hyottoko; the *modoki,* whose function was to ridicule sacred rituals; the *namahage* festival in the North, where young men wearing gruesome masks enter houses with their boots on, shouting and roaring, threatening and frightening children, or pinching the bottoms of brides; and the *akutai matsuri,* where participants use abusive language and gestures against fellow participants and priests" (Viala and Sekine, 15).

Forgotten Garden

1. *Niwa* is structured in this traditional *jo-ha-kyu* manner, as detailed by Susan Blakeley Klein in her analysis of *Niwa.* Susan Blakeley Klein, *Ankoku Buto: The Premodern and Postmodern Influences on the Dance of Utter Darkness* (Ithaca: East Asia Series, Cornell University Press, 1993), 55–68.

2. Ibid., 67

3. Marcia Siegel, "Flickering Stones," *Village Voice*, October 15, 1985.

4. Klein, 63–64.

5. Donna Wilshire, *Virgin, Mother, Crone: Myths and Mysteries of the Triple Goddess*, foreword by Riane Eisler (Rochester, Vt.: Inner Traditions, 1994).

6. Butoh in many cases has improvisational elements, but Butoh artists employ various improvisational processes that are not commensurate with the broad use of the term in modern/postmodern dance. Improvisations in Butoh classes I have taken are similar to the guided/imagistic improvisations I experienced at the Wigman School in Berlin and in my study with Alwin Nikolais who also traces back to Wigman through Hanya Holm.

Shibui and the Sublime

1. Ernst Scheyer, "The Shapes of Space: The Art of Mary Wigman and Oskar Schlemmer," *Dance Perspectives* 41 (spring 1970): 20.

2. J. Hiller, *Japanese Color Prints* (London: Phaidon Press Ltd., 1991), 5–26. Hiller quotes Laurence Binyon and O'Brien Sexton in their belief that as pure design Ukiyo-e is "unrivalled in any other country, unless perhaps by Greek vases," 24.

3. Ibid., 20.

4. Joan Laage, "Embodying the Spirit: The Significance of the Body in the Contemporary Japanese Dance Movement of Butoh," Ph.D. dissertation, Texas Woman's University, August 1993. Laage discusses dance therapist Joan Chodorow's theory of body consciousness at three levels: the personal, the cultural, and the primordial, and the demonstration of these layers in Butoh (66–67).

5. Thomas Huhn, "The Kantian Sublime and the Nostalgia for Violence," *The Journal of Aesthetics and Art Criticism* 53, no. 3 (summer 1995): 269–75.

6. Emmanuel Kant, *Critique of Judgement*, AA. vol. 5., trans. Werner S. Pluhar (Indianapolis: Hackett, 1987), 120–21.

7. Maire Jaanus Kurrik, *Literature and Negation* (New York: Columbia University Press, 1979), 51.

8. David Hume, *A Treatise of Human Nature*, ed. L. A. Selby-Bigge (Oxford: Clarendon, 1888), 436.

9. Judith Butler, *Gender Trouble: Feminism and the Subversion of Identity* (New York: Routledge, 1990).

10. Scheyer, 29.

11. Huhn, 269.

12. Charles Keil reports that the Tiv people of northern Nigeria use the word *wanger* to describe the physical beauty of the body: "wanger means that the body must 'glow' in order to be beautiful," *Tiv Song* (Chicago: University of Chicago Press, 1979), 43. This is directly related to what the Tiv term a "good dancer," as Robert Farris Thompson describes in *African Art in Motion: Icon and Act* (Berkeley: University of California Press, 1974), 44.

13. Thomas Weiskel hypothesizes that the motivation for the romantic sublime stems from the denial of the pre-Oedipal pleasures of the mother's body in *The Romantic Sublime: Studies in the Structure and Psychology of Transcendence* (Baltimore: Johns Hopkins University Press, 1976).

14. Donald Richie, *A Lateral View: Essays on Contemporary Japan*, rev. ed. (Tokyo: Japan Times, Ltd., 1991), 93.

15. Quotations are from Amagatsu's poetry in the program notes.

My Mother's Face

1. The classical work on ecofeminism is Susan Griffin's *Woman and Nature: The Roaring Inside Her* (New York: Harper and Row, 1978). For essays on ecofeminism, see *Reweaving the World: The Emergence of Ecofeminism*, ed. Irene Diamond and Gloria Feman Orenstein (San Francisco: Sierra Club Books, 1990).

2. Maria Gimbutas, *The Language of the Goddess* (San Francisco: Harper and Row, 1989), xix.

3. Female archeomythologists Marija Gimbutas and Riane Eisler are in the forefront of research into prehistoric partnership cultures. Eisler coined the word *gylany* to stand for the cultural equality of men and women. *Gyne* stands for woman and *andros* for man. The letter *l* links them. See Eisler, *The Chalice and the Blade* (San Francisco: Harper and Row, 1987). See also Gimbutas, *The Goddesses and Gods of Old Europe* (Berkeley and Los Angeles: University of California Press, 1982).

4. Donna Wilshire's book, *Virgin, Mother, Crone: Myths and Mysteries of the Triple Goddess* (Rochester, Vt.: Inner Traditions, 1994), provides a fuller explanation of goddess-based values and aesthetics. In its own way, Butoh dances forth the three faces of the Goddess that Wilshire researches and praises with creative hymns.

Shards

1. Saburo Teshigawara, quoted by Marilyn Hunt in "Teshigawara: Violent Beauty," *Dance Magazine* (April 1991): 50–53.

2. Ibid.

3. Marilyn Hunt, "Teshigawara: Violent Beauty."

Liebe

1. This is a twenty-minute film now located in the Dance Collection of the New York City Public Library. Besides our performances for Wigman's birthday, it includes samples of the class work at the school: composition and technique classes with Wigman, a technique class with guest teacher Helmut Gottschild, "gymnasic" and pantomime with Til Thiele, and a music class with Herr Kessler. I also have a video copy of the film.

2. Susan Blakeley Klein, *Ankoku Buto: The Premodern and Postmodern Influences on the Dance of Utter Darkness* (Ithaca: East Asia Series, Cornell University Press, 1988), 7. Also stated in Ohno's vita.

Beginner's Body

1. Kayo Mikami, *The Body as Vessel: Tatsumi Hijikata—An Approach to the Techniques of Ankoku-Butoh* (Tokyo: ANZ-Do Publications, 1993).
2. Shunryu Suzuki, *Zen Mind, Beginner's Mind*, 28th ed. (New York: Weatherhill, 1991; 1st ed., 1970), 14, 21.

Hokohtai: The Walking Body

1. Soto Zen favorite saying, as recounted by Daisetz Teitaro Suzuki in *The Field of Zen*, ed. with foreword by Christmas Humphreys (New York: Perennial Library, Harper and Row, 1969), 71.

The Hanging Body

1. This essay is based on *Nothing Lasts but Memory*, performed at State University of New York, College at Brockport, April 23, 1994, and on conversations with Joan Laage April 24–26, 1994, and November 3, 1994.

Zen and Wabi-Sabi Taste

1. Leonard Koren, *Wabi-Sabi for Artists, Designers, Poets and Philosophers* (Berkeley, Calif.: Stone Bridge Press, 1994), 42–45.
2. Ibid., 22, 31.
3. Donald Richie, *A Lateral View: Essays on Contemporary Japan*, rev. ed. (Tokyo: Japan Times, Ltd., 1991), 95.
4. Koren, 21–22.
5. Susan Blakeley Klein has also seen the Zen Buddhist influences on Butoh. See *Ankoku Buto: The Premodern and Postmodern Influences on the Dance of Utter Darkness* (Ithaca: East Asia Series, Cornell University Press, 1988), 67.

6. See *The Secret of the Golden Flower: The Classic Chinese Book of Life*, trans. Thomas Cleary (San Francisco: Harper San Francisco, 1991).

7. Yuriko Saito, "The Japanese Aesthetics of Imperfection and Insufficiency," *The Journal of Aesthetics and Art Criticism* 55, no. 4 (fall 1997): 377–85, 382.

8. Kenko Yoshida, *Essays in Idleness: The Tsurezureguza of Kenko*, trans. Donald Keene (New York: Columbia University Press, 1967), 7.

The Community Body

1. There is a therapy called Korper Kontact, developed as a system of physical contact through Butoh sensibilities.

Selected
Bibliography

Ashihara, Eiryo. *The Japanese Dance*. Tokyo: Japan Travel Bureau, 1964.

Barthes, Roland. *Empire of Signs*. Trans. Richard Howard. New York: Hill and Wang; Farrar, Straus, and Giroux, 1982.

Blackwood, Michael. *Butoh: Body on the Edge of Crisis*. Michael Blackwood Productions, video, 1990.

Caldwell, Helen. *Michio Ito: The Dancer and His Dances*. Berkeley: University of California Press, 1977.

Cleary, Thomas, trans. *The Secret of the Golden Flower: The Classic Chinese Book of Life*. San Francisco: Harper San Francisco, 1991.

Cowell, Mary-Jean, with Satoru Simazaki. "East and West in the Work of Michio Ito." *Dance Research Journal* 26, no. 2 (fall 1994): 11–22.

Hiller, J. *Japanese Color Prints*. London: Phaidon Press Ltd., 1991.

Hoff, Frank. "Killing the Self: How the Narrator Acts." *Asian Theatre Journal* 2, no. 1 (spring 1985): 1–25.

Hoffman, Yoel, ed. *Japanese Death Poems Written by Zen Monks and Haiku Poets on the Verge of Death*. Rutland, Vt. and Tokyo, Japan: Charles E. Tuttle Co., 1986.

Huhn, Thomas. "The Kantian Sublime and the Nostalgia for Violence." *The Journal of Aesthetics and Art Criticism* 53, no. 3 (summer 1995): 269–75.

Humphreys, Christmas, ed. *The Field of Zen*. New York: Perennial Library, Harper and Row, 1969.

Hunt, Marilyn. "Teshigawara: Violent Beauty." *Dance Magazine* (April 1991): 50–53.

Ichikawa, Miyabi. "Butoh: The Denial of the Body." *Ballet International* 12, no. 12 (September 1989): 14–17.

Ives, Colta Feller. *The Great Wave: The Influence of Japanese Woodcuts on French Prints*. New York: Metropolitan Museum of Art, 1974.

Kasai, Akira. "Dance Closely Related to Matter." *Nikutaemo: Butoh Dance Bilingual Journal* 2 (summer 1996): 19–39.

Kellermann, Bernhard. *Japanische Tanze*. Berlin: Paul Cassirer, Verlag, 1920.

Kenko, Yoshida. *Essays in Idleness: The Tsurezuregusa of Kenko*. Trans. Donald Keene. New York: Columbia University Press, 1967.

Kisselgoff, Anna. "Review of Dai Rakuda Kan." *New York Times*, April 19, 1987.

Klein, Susan Blakeley. *Ankoku Buto: The Premodern and Postmodern Influences on the Dance of Utter Darkness*. Ithaca: East Asia Series, Cornell University Press, 1988.

Koren, Lenord. *Wabi-Sabi for Artists, Designers, Poets and Philosophers*. Berkeley: Stone Bridge Press, 1994.

Kozel, Susan. "Moving Beyond the Double Syntax." *Dance Theatre Journal* 13, no. 1 (summer 1996): 36–37.

Laage, Joan. "Embodying the Spirit: The Significance of the Body in the Contemporary Japanese Dance Movement of Butoh." Ph.D. dissertation, Texas Woman's University, Denton, Texas, 1993.

Lebra, Takie Sugiyama, and William P. Lebra, eds. *Japanese Culture and Behavior*. Honolulu: University Press of Hawaii, 1974.

Matida, Kasyo. *Odori (Japanese Dance)*. Board of Tourist Industry and Japanese Government Railways, 1938.

O'Neill, P. G. *A Guide to No*. Tokyo: Hinoki Shoten, 1953.

Philip, Richard, and Bonnie Sue Stein. "Out of Darkness: Butoh," Parts I and II. *Dance Magazine* (April 1986): 60–68.

Reischauer, Edwin O. *The Japanese*. Cambridge: Harvard University Press, 1977.

Richie, Donald. *A Lateral View: Essays on Contemporary Japan*. Rev. ed. Tokyo: Japan Times, Ltd., 1991.

Rotie, Marie-Gabrielle. "The Re-orientation of Butoh." *Dance Theatre Journal* 13, no. 1 (spring 1996): 34-35.

Saito, Yuriko. "The Japanese Aesthetics of Imperfection and Insufficiency." *The Journal of Aesthetics and Art Criticism* 55, no. 4 (fall 1997): 377-85.

Scheyer, Ernst. "The Shapes of Space: The Art of Mary Wigman and Oskar Schlemmer." *Dance Perspectives* 41 (New York: Dance Perspectives Foundation, 1970).

Siegel, Marcia. "Flickering Stones." *Village Voice* 15 (October 1985).

Singer, Kurt. *Mirror, Sword and Jewel: A Study of Japanese Characteristics.* Introduction by Richard Storry. New York: George Braziller, 1973.

Smith, Gradley. *Japan: A History in Art.* New York: Simon and Schuster, 1964.

Stein, Bonnie Sue. "Butoh." *The Drama Review* 30 (summer 1986): 107-70.

———. "Twenty Years Ago We Were Crazy, Dirty and Mad." *The Drama Review* 30, no. 2 (summer 1986): 107-26.

Suzuki, Shunryu. *Zen Mind, Beginner's Mind.* New York: Weatherhill, 1991.

Takeo, Kuwabara. *Japan and Western Civilization: Essays on Comparative Culture.* Trans. Kano Tsutomu and Patricia Murray, ed. Kato Hidetoshi. Tokyo: University of Tokyo Press, 1983.

Viala, Jean, and Nourit Masson Sekine. *Butoh: Shades of Darkness.* Tokyo: Shufunotomo Co. Ltd., 1988.

Warner, Langdon. *The Enduring Art of Japan.* Cambridge: Harvard University Press, 1958.

Weiskel, Thomas. *The Romantic Sublime: Studies in the Structure and Psychology of Transcendence.* Baltimore: Johns Hopkins University Press, 1976.

Wigman, Mary. *The Language of Dance.* Trans. Walter Sorrell. London: MacDonald and Evans, 1966.

Yuasa, Yasuo. *The Body.* Trans. Nagatomo Shigenori and T. P. Kasulis, ed. T. P. Kasulis. Albany: State University of New York Press, 1987.

Index

Note: Page numbers for illustrations are in italics.

Affecte (Linke), 126–34, *131*
Affectos Humanos (Hoyer), 128–29, *130*
Akane, Akiko, 21–22, 60, 153, 164;
  family of, 166–69
Akane, Mrs., 168–70
Akane-sensei, Shodo, 26, 168–69, 185;
  on Zen, 181, 214
Alexander, F. M., 64
All Moonshine (Yoshioka), 241–45
Amagatsu, Ushio, 34, 38, *204*; and
  Jomon Sho (Homage to Prehistory),
  81–86; and Sankai Juku dance com-
  pany, 67–71
Amaterasu (Great Goddess), 58
American dance, 31–32, 45–46
Ando, Mitsuko, 32
*Are We Carrying Our Bodies into the World of
  the Dead?* (Kasai), 229
Ariadone company, 243
Art, Japanese, 11–12, 70, 253n19
Ashida, Sachio, 201–02
Ashikawa, Akeno, *179*
Ashikawa, Yoko, *2*, *14*, *154*; and *hoko-
  htai* (walking body), 177–78; style
  of, 29–30, 38, 176; workshops by,
  139, 141–49, 218
Association of American Theater in
  Higher Education, 15
Astaire, Fred, 158–59
Attention/focus, 18, 200

Audience, involvement in Butoh, 51,
  142, 176, 245
Avant garde theater, 11–12

Balanchine, George, 76–77, 251n2
Ballet, 31, 40, 79, 128; Butoh blended
  with, 220, 239; compared to Butoh,
  66, 173, 224; rejection of, 76–78
Baryshnikov, 158–59
Basho, 150
Bausch, Pina, 8, 73–74, *75*, 78–79;
  Sankai Juku company contrasted
  with, 66, 68–70
Beckett, Samuel, 232
Biwa-Kei dance company, 219
Body, 84–85, 98, 154, 196, 213; bal-
  let's rejection of, 76–78; in Butoh,
  38, 173, 175–76, 235; community,
  42, 229–31, 236–37, 247–49;
  "killing," 25, 88, 92, 233, 239; in
  modern women's dance themes,
  52–53; as theme in Butoh, 42,
  63–64, 71; and types of sublimity,
  78–81
Body as Vessel, The: Tatsumi Hijikata
  (Mikami), 140
Bowing, 51, 116, 120
Broellin Castle, 243–45
Buddhism, 25, 51, 81. *See also* Zen
Butler, Judith, 74

Butoh, 15, 22–23, 98–99, 134, 204; blended with other traditions, 15, 36, 38–42, 81, 220; catharsis through, 14, 25, 34, 138; darkness of, 3, 58, 94, 175; dropping sand in, 225–26; evolution of, 6–9, 12–13, 23, 140, 175, 230; expressionism in, 34, 36, 125; feminism in, 52, 94–95; founders of, 127–28, 230–31, 233; improvisation in, 54, 256n6; internationalism of, 14, 24, 30, 42; killing the body in, 229–30; movement in, 64, 177–78, 218, 223, 235; nature of, 2–6, 28, 80, 166–67, 224–25, 236; Noh compared to, 171–73; relation to Zen, 43–44; similarity of *Nothing Lasts but Memory* to, 210–12; *Solo 1* as, 196–98; teaching, 140–42; values of, 3, 14, 23–24, 46, 93, 199; variety in, 38, 58
Butoh Festival (San Francisco), 228–45

Campbell, Joseph, 52
Candle Dancers (Nolde), 69
Catharsis, 30, 125; through Butoh, 14, 25, 34, 138
Chandralekha, 126
Chanting, and Zen meditation, 21–22
Choreography, 35, 116, 182; Butoh, 6, 54, 67, 98, 145–47, 235; in Japanese modern dance, 31–32
Clytemnestra (Graham), 35
Community body, 42, 229–31, 236–37, 247–49
Concert dance. *See* Modern dance, Japanese
Congress on Research on Dance, 15
Consciousness, in Butoh dancing, 85, 245
Corpses, Butoh use of bodies as, 235
Costumes: in *All Moonshine*, 243; in Butoh, 6, 11, 23–24; for *Forests, Gathering Honey of the Moon*, 222, 224; in *Ishi-No-Hana (Flower of Stone)*, 99; in

Kasai's improvisation, 240–41; in *Liebe*, 135; in *Niwa (The Garden)*, 46, 48–49; *Nothing Lasts but Memory*, 210; in *Sleep and Reincarnation From Empty Land*, 106–10, 112, 114–16; in *Solo 1*, 196–97; in *Tree IV*, 155, 161–62
Crandall, David, 212
Creation myths, 29
Crump, Juliette, 164
Crystal Vagina, The (Yamada), 220
Cunningham, Merce, 63, 126, 128, 182

Daily life, as theme of Ukiyo-e, 10
Dairakudakan (Butoh company), 26–28, 27
Dalcroze Technique, 31–32
Dance concerts, student, 118
Dance dramas, 35–36
Dance education, 18
Dance theater, 6, 32
Dance therapy, 36, 42–43, 256n4
Dancers' Group (San Francisco), 14, 228
De Beauvoir, Simone, 126
Death, 68, 94; in *Rites of Spring*, 74, 75; as theme in Butoh, 6, 14
Denishawn school, 33
Dairakudakan Butoh company, 26–28, 27, 143
Die Brucke, 69
Dietrich, Urs, 127, 129, 132–34
D-net, 14
Dogen Zen, 25, 141, 214–15, 218
Dream of the Fetus, A (Ohno), 13
Dreh Monotonie (Fraleigh), 253n16
Duncan, Isadora, 24, 76, 85, 236, 238; Nakajima compared to, 46, 52
Dunning, Jennifer, 41

East/West, 32, 40; differences in, 68–70, 203, 231, 233–34; Eastern influences on modern dance, 254n21, 255n24; influences on Butoh, 23–24, 51, 98, 105, 126; integration of, 8–9, 252n8; and Kantian sublime, 71–73

Ego: in Butoh, 42, 238; dancer's, 182–83, 249; and freedom *vs.* integration, 199–200; letting go of, 88, 92; in Zen, 200–02

Eguchi, Takaya, 31–32, 127–28; influence of, 34, 253n18

Eiko, 15

Eisler, Riane, 258n3

Emotions: in Butoh, 25, 45–46, 98, 142–43; in dance, 63, 85–86, 128–29, 134; in Ukiyo-e and Butoh, 11, 13; in Zen Dance, 202

Emptiness. *See Mu* (emptiness)

Empty Land. See Sleep and Reincarnation From Empty Land (Nakajima)

Endicott, Josephine, 74

Ensor, James, 68

Eroticism, as theme in Butoh, 61

Eurythmy, 230, 239

Existentialism, 126–27, 141, 184–85, 252n8

Expressionism, 8, 12; of Bausch and Sankai Juku company, 68–70; and Butoh, 23–25, 34, 98; in dance, 35, 85, 124; influence on modern dance, 8–9, 31–32, 128. *See also* German expressionism

Facial expressions: in Butoh, 11, 154; in Kasai's improvisation, 239–40; in *Niwa (The Garden)*, 46–48, 50–51; in *Sleep and Reincarnation From Empty Land*, 106, 111

Fauvism, and European expressionism, 69

Feldenkrais, Moshe, 64

Feminine, 72, 126; in ballet, 76–77; brutalized, 70, 79; in Butoh, 3, 13, 52; in dance dramas, 35–36; and mother, 90–96; in Ohno's teaching, 57–58

Festival of New Dance, 45–54, 81

Flock Descends Into the Pentagonal Garden, A (Takamitsu), 203

Fokine, Michel, 254n21

Forests, Gathering Honey of the Moon (Yamada), 219–27

Fraleigh, Sondra, 167, 193

Frazer, Kathleen, 251n2

Freedom, 62; as theme, 142, 198; through dance, 184–85; *vs.* integration, 199–200

Freedom and Nature (Ricouer), 184

Gender, 58, 95; as merging of nature and culture, 73–74; yin/yang of, 90–91

Genet, Jean, 174

German dance: and Butoh, 38–40, 243; modern, 31–32; use of Japanese stylization: modern dance, 40

German expressionism, 13, 24–25, 127; and Butoh, 7, 36, 232, 235; and dance, 66, 124, 134

Gesamtkunstwerk (total theater), 69–70

Ghosts, as theme, 162

Gimbutas, Marija, 258n3

Glass, Philip, 203

Goda, Nario, 80, 142–43, 153; interview with, 171–76

Goddess, 51, 90–96, 258n4

Gottschild, Brenda Dixon, 251n2

Graham, Martha, 8, 13, 25, 31, 35, 40; Nakajima compared to, 41–42, 52; use of Japanese stylization, 40, 254n20

Greek mythology, 35–36, 40

Greek tragedy, 25, 142

Gunji, Masakatsu, 15

Gunji, Masakatsu, 43

Haiku, 150, 162, 168; from Ashikawa's classes, 148–49; of everyday things, 180–81; on Japan, 186–94; on *Tree IV*, 156–57

Hakutobo dance company, 179

Hara, N., 73

Hardy, Camille, 2

Harunobu, Suzuki, 10

Harushige, 10

Hawk-Moth and Butterflies (Shunman), 13
"Head of anxiety *Onnagata*" (Shunko), 10
Healing, Butoh as, 237, 245
Here to Here (Teshigawara), 99
Herstad, Monica Emilie, 14
Hideyoshe, Toyotomi, 216–17
Hijikata, Tatsumi, 4, 12, 94, 172; background of, 32, 173–74; as founder of Butoh, 6–8, 13–14, 175, 230–31, 237, 252n15; influence of, 11–12, 236, 246; students of, 112, 140, 144, 233, 241, 246; style of, 11, 29–30, 38, 64, 95, 231
Hijikata Triptych (La Bobgah), 6, 7
Hirata, Mikio, 231
Hocutobo dance company, 140, 176
Hoko (Butoh walk), 143–47
Hokohtai (walking body), 143–47, 177–78
Holm, Hanya, 25
Homosexuality (*Kinjinki*), 174
Hoyer, Dora, 124, 130, 253n16; death of, 127–28; Linke's tribute to, 125, 127
Huhn, Thomas, 72, 77
Hume, David, 72
Humie (author's Japanese daughter), 118–23
Humphrey, Doris, 31, 33, 52

Improvisations, 252n9; Butoh as, 43, 54, 256n6; by Kasai, 230, 238, 247–49; in workshops, 36–38, 60–62, 64, 87–88, 141, 144–49, 164–65, 247–49
India, 26
Ishii, Baku, 31–32, 253n18
Ishi-No-Hana (Flower of Stone) (Teshigawara), 98–103, 101
Itako town, Japan, 119–22
Ito, Michio, 32–33
Iwashita, Toru, 42–43, 124–25, 134–38, 136, 137

Japan, 3, 253n19; aesthetics of, 58–59, 216, 227; art, 11–12, 70, 253n19;
and Butoh, 43, 173; Butoh as expression of, 3–4, 14, 23, 40; culture of, 51, 58, 118, 199–200, 203–04; expressionism in, 68–69; folk identity of, 4, 9; and modern dance, 41–42, 182; prose and haiku on, 186–94; response to Butoh in, 15, 24; reverence for nature in, 96, 237. *See also* Modern dance, Japanese
Jo image, 47–48
Jomon Sho (Homage to Prehistory) (Amagatsu), 71, 81–86, 83
Jooss, Kurt, 13, 68
Judo, 17–18, 201

Ka Cho Fu Getsu (Ohno), 162
Kabuki Butoh "Jesus Christ in Aomori" (Gungi), 15, 16
Kabuki theater, 24, 34, 186; influence of, 81–82, 105, 246; movement in, 58–59; relation of Butoh to, 9–11, 15, 40
Kanai, Fumie, 33–34, 182
Kantian sublime, 65–67, 71–73, 81. *See also* Sublimity
Karaoke, 120–21, 135
"Karaoke expressionism," 124
Karas dance company, 103
Kasai, Akira, 42, 228–41, 229, 234, 247–49
Kasai, Mitsu, 229
Kawaguchi, Chio, 153
Kenka (Consecration of Flowers) (Mikami), 38, 39, 143
Kinjiki cycle (Hijikata), 4–6
Kinjinki (homosexuality), 174
Kirchner, Ernst, 69
Kiyomine, Torii, 10
Kiyotada, Torii, 252n15
Klein, Susan, 51
Kokoschka, Oskar, 70
Koma, 15
Korean Zen, 202
Kreutzberg, Harald, 13, 68, 128, 253n18
Kurrick, Maire, 72

La Bobgah, Robert, 6–7
Laage, Joan, 8, 209–13, 210, 213, 256n4
Laban, Rudolph von, 222–23, 236
Lee, Sun Ok, 202
Liebe (Love) (Hoyer), 124
Liebe (Love) (Iwashita), 124, 134–38, 136, 137
Liebe (Love) (Linke), 124–25
Light/darkness: in *All Moonshine*, 241; in Butoh, 173–75; in *Forests, Gathering Honey of the Moon*, 226; in *Jomon Sho (Homage to Prehistory)*, 82–84; in *Liebe*, 135, 138; and Mother Goddess, 94–96; in *Niwa (The Garden)*, 47–48; in *Nothing Lasts but Memory*, 210–11; in *Sleep and Reincarnation From Empty Land*, 106; in *Solo 1*, 196; and types of sublimity, 79–80
Lilac Garden (Yamada), 220
Linke, Susanne, 8, 124–34, 131, 133
Literature, influence on dance dramas, 3, 35
Literature and Negation (Kurrick), 72
Love, 53, 92; as theme in dance, 124–25
Lyricism, in Japanese modern dance, 33

Maezawa, Yuriko, 46, 48
Magito, Victor, 41, 254n22
Maple Leaf Monastery, 21–22
Marble Bath, The, 55–56
Martial arts, 18
Masamura, Katsuko, 32
Masks, 43, 49; white face as, 104–05; Wigman's use of, 35, 41, 254n22
Matsumoto-sensei, Chiyoe, 18–19, 20
Meditation: *hokohtai* as, 177–78; Zen, 20–22, 200, 202, 218
Meiji period, in Japan's avant garde theater, 11–12
Mikami, Kayo, 8, 29–30, 38, 39, 139–40, 143
Mind, 77, 195; influence on Butoh, 142–43; over nature, 65, 67, 71–73
Mind/body relationship, 25–28, 213, 218–19, 235
Minimalism, 6, 204–06, 216

Mishima, 174
Mito City, Japan, 117–19
Miya, Souko, 253n18
Miyaki, Issey, 204
Miyata, Kei, 100
Modern dance, 31; Butoh's links to, 8, 38–40, 51–52; Eastern influence on, 8, 40, 255n24; emotions in, 13, 124–25; evolution of, 41–42, 128; Japanese, 30–34, 40–42, 182. *See also* German dance
Mother, 78; discovering through dance, 88–96; in improvisations, 164–65; as theme in Butoh, 61, 64
Mother Goddess, 93–94
Moths, as subject, 13
Movement, 37–38; in *Affecte*, 132; in *All Moonshine*, 243; in Butoh, 58–59, 64; of Butoh walks, 143–47, 177–78; in *Dreh Monotonie*, 253n16; in *Forests, Gathering Honey of the Moon*, 222–24; freedom through, 184–85; in improvisations, 62, 239–40; in *Ishi-No-Hana (Flower of Stone)*, 99–100; in *Jomon Sho (Homage to Prehistory)*, 82, 85–86; in *Niwa (The Garden)*, 47, 50–51; in *Sleep and Reincarnation From Empty Land*, 106–10, 114–16; in *Solo 1*, 197–98; in *Suiren*, 161–62; in *Tree IV*, 155
Mu (emptiness), 14, 44, 203
Murder, Hope of Women (Kokoschka), 70
Music, 59, 203; in *Affecte*, 132; in Butoh, 23, 176; for improvisations, 62, 239; in *Ishi-No-Hana (Flower of Stone)*, 99; in *Liebe*, 135; in *Niwa (The Garden)*, 47, 51; in *Rites of Spring*, 74; in *Shijima (The Darkness Calms Down in Space)*, 204; in *Sleep and Reincarnation From Empty Land*, 105, 111, 115; in *Solo 1*, 198; sounds in *Forests, Gathering Honey of the Moon*, 219–20; in *Suiren*, 161–62
My Mother (Ohno), 2, 58, 62–64
Mythology: Greek, 35–36, 40; Mother Goddess in, 90–91, 93; religious, 182

Nagareru Kubi (Ashikawa), 177–78

Nakajima, Natsu, 2–3, 15, 42, 113, 140; in *Niwa (The Garden)*, 45–54, 49, 50; and Ohno, 59–61, 63; performance in NY, 104–16; style of, 29–30, 38, 41–42, 154; workshops by, 87–88, 92, 218

Nakamura, Kyozo, 15

Nature, 79, 86, 149, 170, 246; and Butoh, 94–95, 237; and Kantian sublime, 65–67, 71–73; movement in, 184–85; reverence for, 96, 105, 123; as theme in Butoh, 11, 23, 64, 70–73

Neo-expressionism, 9, 124

Neue Tanz, 31

Nietzsche, Friedrich Wilhelm, 68, 142, 252n8

Night Journey (Graham), 35

Nijinsky, Vaslav, 236, 238–39

Niwa (The Garden) (Nakajima), 45–54, 49, 50, 111

Noguchi, Isamu, 40

Noh dance-drama, 24, 34, 43, 204; compared to Butoh, 81–82, 105, 171–73; masks of, 40–41; movement in, 58–59, 145

NOIJECT (Teshigawara), 99

Nolde, Emil, 69

Nothing Lasts but Memory (Laage), 209–13

Nudity, 23–24, 152–54

Ohno, Kazuo, 2, 7, 13, 43, 57–64, 85, 92, 160, 165; author's introduction to, 54, 59–61; background of, 32, 34, 128, 253n18; as founder of Butoh, 6, 13–14, 230–32, 237; and Kasai, 230, 233, 241; style of, 24, 30, 38, 64, 95, 126, 140, 158–60; as teacher, 60–63, 97–98, 212, 233; workshops by, 36–38, 164–65, 218

Ohno, Yoshito, 4, 7, 161–62, 165

Ohno village, Japan, 120–23

O-kub-e (large heads), 10

Old Man and the Sea (Ohno), 232

Omikami Amaterasu (Great Sun Goddess), 58, 96, 105

Oriental stereotypes, 32, 254n21. *See also* East/West

"Other": enrichment through, 1, 17; flesh as, 78; mutual differences caused by, 20–22

Perspective, in Tanaka's dance, 154–55

Photography, 6, 19

Piazzolla, Astor, 198

"Pictures of the Floating World School." *See* Ukiyo-e

Play, as theme, 10–11

Poe Project, The cycle (Tanaka), 3

Pop art, in Japan, 12

Post-Butohism, 6, 9, 98, 224

Postmodern dance: American: influence of Butoh on, 15; similarities with Butoh, 23; influence on Butoh, 6

Postmodernism: Butoh as, 38; in dance of Teshigawara, 98; fragmentation in, 33; reflected through Butoh, 3–4, 8–9

Ra'i, Delta, 245

Rainer, Yvonne, 128

Rebellion of the Body, The (Hijikata), 174

Rebellion of the Body (Hijikata), 94

Redlich, Don, 25

Reversibility: of polarized elements, 29; and ritual inversions, 43, 255n26

Revolt of the Flesh (Hijikata), 11

Rice powder. *See* White powder

Richie, Donald, 12, 80

Ricouer, Paul, 184

Rikyu, Sen no, 216–17

Rites of Spring (Bausch), 73–74, 75

Roses (Taylor), 33

Rosy Dance, 231

Rouault, Georges, 69

Saito, Yuriko, 227

Sankai Juku dance company, 34, 65–68,

124, 128, 204–06, 226; critique of, 175–76; and sublimity, 79–86
Sato, Midori, 64–65
Scheyer, Ernst, 40–41, 254n22
Schlemmer, Oskar, 69, 77
Schoenberg, Arnold, 203
Seigel, Marcia, 52
Self-inquiry, 202
Seraphita (Kasai), 230
Sets, 6, 40; for *Forests, Gathering Honey of the Moon*, 219; for *Jomon Sho: Homage to Prehistory*, 81, 84; for Kasai's improvisations, 240–41; for *Solo 1*, 196
Sex, as theme, 11, 174
Shawn, Ted, 254n21
Shibui (restraint), 66, 70, 80–86
Shijima (*The Darkness Calms Down in Space*) (Sankai Juku), 204–06, 205
Shintoism, 4, 51; love of nature in, 96, 105, 246; shrines, 122–23
Showa period, in Japan's avant garde theater, 11–12
Shuko, Murata, 216
Shunko, Katsukawa, 10
Shunman, Kobu, 13
Sleep and Reincarnation From Empty Land (Nakajima), 54, 105–16, 109, 113, 115
Sleep and Reincarnation (Graham), 41–42
Solo 1 (Van der Pluijm), 195–98
Son (Korean Zen), 202
Soto Zen, 235
St. Denis, Ruth, 8, 52, 254n21
Stage locations: in Butoh solos, 135; in *Forests, Gathering Honey of the Moon*, 224; in *Niwa* (*The Garden*), 47–48; in *Sleep and Reincarnation From Empty Land*, 107, 111
Steiner, Rudolf, 230
Streb, Elizabeth, 17–18
Structure, in Japanese modern dance, 33
Subjects, 32–33; for Butoh, 30, 34; for improvisations, 37–38, 252n9; of Ukiyo-e and Butoh, 9–10. *See also* Nature

Sublimity, 51, 66; in ballet, 76–77; romantic, 66, 257n13; types of, 78–81. *See also* Kantian sublime
Suiren (*Waterlily*) (Ohno), 159–62, 160
Surrealism, influence on Hijikata, 232
Suzuki, Shunru, 44
Suzuki, Shunryu, 141
Symbolism, in Butoh, 232

Tai chai, 220, 222–23
Taisho period, 11–12
Taisho-look, 12–13, 28
Takamitsu, Toru, 203
Takashi, Kogo, 21
Takei, Kei, 15, 98
Talbot, Valerie, 54
Tale of the Supernatural Sea Dappled Horse, 26–28
Tanaka, Min, 3, 6, 38, 152–54, 153, 175
Tanztheater, 8, 68
Taoism, "The Way" in, 25
Tatoeba-Theatre Danse Grotesque, 243–45
Taylor, Paul, 33
Tea ceremony, 18–19, 170, 204, 216
Tensi-Kan dance school and company, 230
Terasaki, Sho, 229
Teshigawara, Saburo, 97–103, 101
Theater, 47. *See also* Gesamtkunstwerk (total theater)
Theater dance, Japanese, 34
Thiele, Mathilde, 127–28
"Third eye," 25–26
Thornbrugh, David, 212
Time, 23, 81; Butoh's, 232; in *Forests, Gathering Honey of the Moon*, 222, 225–26; in Zen Dance, 181–83, 203
Tomozoe, Heidenori, 17–18, 201–02
Transformations: in Butoh, 29, 154; in *Niwa* (*The Garden*), 51; in *Suiren*, 161–62; and *wabi-sabi*, 215
Tree IV Installation (Tanaka), 152–54
Triadic Ballet (Schlemmer), 69

Tsu, Lao, 217
Tsubaki Shrine, 122–23

Ukiyo-e (Japanese prints), 8–11; compared to Butoh, 11, 13, 40, 71; Japanese expressionism in, 68–69; popularity of, 253n19, 254n20
Ukiyo-e (Kiyotada), 252n15
Unconscious, influence on dance dramas, 35
U.S.: fascination with Japan in, 40; modern dance in, 31–32

Van der Pluijm, Annamirl, 195–98, 197
Violence, 72–74, 77

Wabi-sabi, 86, 94, 214–17, 219–27
Waguri, Yukio, 15, 105–07, 110, 116, 252n9
Waiting for Godot, 232
Waterlilies (Ohno), 24
Weidman, Charles, 254n21
Weiskel, Thomas, 257n13
West, 9, 11. See also East/West
White powder: on bodies, 71, 82; on faces, 11, 41, 46, 104, 106, 196
Wiatowitsch, Dimitri, 132
Wigman, Mary, 8, 13, 31; Butoh's similarity to, 235–36; dance dramas of, 35–36; expressionism of, 68, 85; influence of, 31, 127, 253nn16,18; influences on, 40–41, 254n22; Nakajima compared to, 46, 51–52. See also Wigman School

Wigman School, 24–25, 36–38, 60–61, 125
Wilshire, Donna, 52–53, 258n4
Wind and Wood (Kanai), 34
Witch Dance (Wigman), 35, 41, 51–52, 68, 236

Yamada, Kosaku, 31, 219–27, 221
Yamada, Setsuko, 6
Yamaguchi, Sayoko, 99, 101
Yas-Kas, 204
Yin/yang, 29, 32; of gender, 3, 90–91, 93; of movement, 110–11, 223
Yoga, 26–29
Yoshikawa, Yoichiro, 204
Yoshioka, Yumiko, 42, 241–46, 242, 244
Yumoto Hakone temple, 21–22

Zazen, 200
Zen, 28, 43, 149; author looking for teacher, 168; beauty in, 214–15; beginner's mind of, 141; Butoh's relation to, 28, 43–44; and dance, 178, 180–85, 202; ego in, 200–01; influence on Butoh, 3–4, 14, 51; koan of, 217–18; nature in, 96, 105, 170, 246; similarities to Butoh, 24, 199; temples, 183; values of, 26, 81, 84, 200, 204, 227. See also Dogen Zen; Meditation
Zen Dance, 202–03